HOW TO DRAW
Book For Kids

This book belongs to

....

....

Hello, the little dreamer!
Let's draw, giggle, and dream together!

Chloe Felix, a beloved author, brings joy to children with her engaging books. Her work inspires and ignites children's boundless imaginations and promotes skills development through delightful and educational content, nurturing a love for learning, creativity, and positive values.

CHLOE FELIX

Disclaimer:
The information and instructions provided in this book are intended to be used as a general guide for drawing. This book is not intended to be a substitute for professional instruction or advice. The reader should always seek the advice of a qualified professional before attempting any new technique or project. The author and publisher disclaim any liability or loss incurred in connection with the use or application of the information and techniques presented in this book.

TABLE OF CONTENTS

Animals

Foods, Fruits & Plants

Acorn	35		Fried Egg	42
Almonds	35		Grape	42
Apple	35		Honey	42
Apricot	35		Hot Chocolate	43
Avocado	35		Hot Dog	43
Banana	36		Ice Cream	43
Bell Pepper	36		Jackfruit	43
Blueberry	36		Jam	44
Bread	36		Kiwi	44
Broccoli	36		Leaf	44
Burger	37		Lemon	44
Burrito	37		Lemonade	45
Cactus	37		Lettuce	45
Candy	37		Lollipop	45
Carrot	37		Macaroon	45
Cheese	38		Mango	46
Cheese Cake	38		Mangosteen	46
Cherry	38		Marshmallow	46
Chili Pepper	38		Milkshake	46
Chips	38		Muffin	47
Chocolate Bar	39		Mushroom	47
Clover	39		Noodles	47
Coconut	39		Onion	47
Cookie	39		Orange	48
Corn	39		Oreo	48
Cotton Candy	40		Palm Tree	48
Crepe	40		Pancake	48
Croissant	40		Panna Cotta	49
Cucumber	40		Papaya	49
Cupcake	40		Passion Fruit	49
Dandelion	41		Peach	49
Donut	41		Peanut	50
Dragonfruit	41		Pear	50
Durian	41		Pineapple	50
Egg Plant	41		Pizza	50
French Fries	42		Pomegranate	51
French Toast	42		Popcorn	51

Foods, Fruits & Plants

Toys, Vehicles & Outer Space

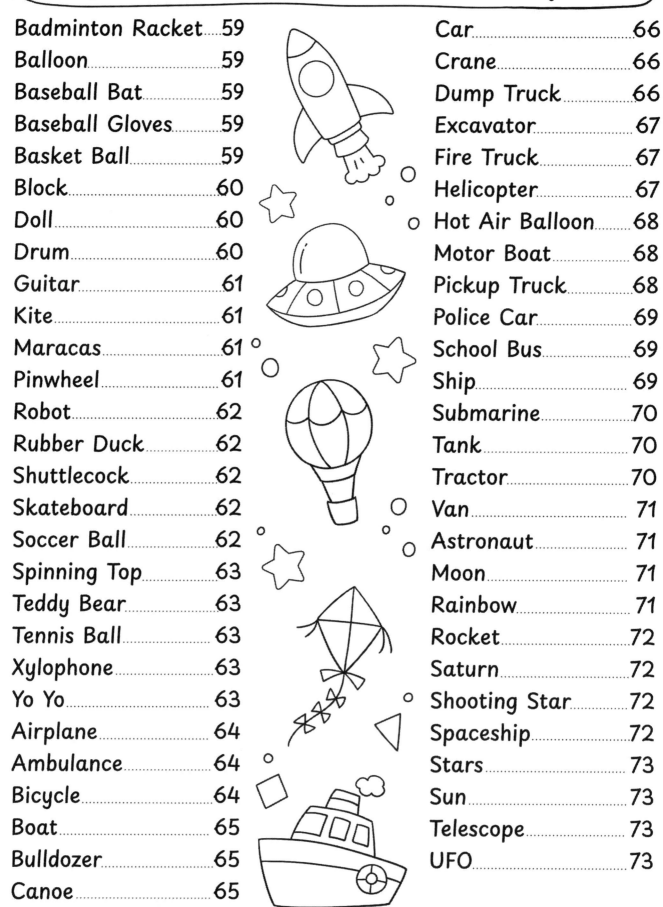

Celebration

Amazing Things

How to Use This Book

Each drawing in this book has two types of lines: Black lines and grey lines.

- Every step in your drawing adventure begins with black lines. They are the most important lines in each step.

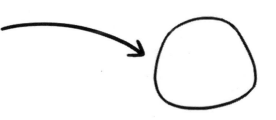

- So, when you see black lines, you should draw exactly what they show you.

- The grey lines are just there to help you see what you've already drawn. It's like a guide to show you where you're at in the drawing process.

So, grab your pencils and let's get started!

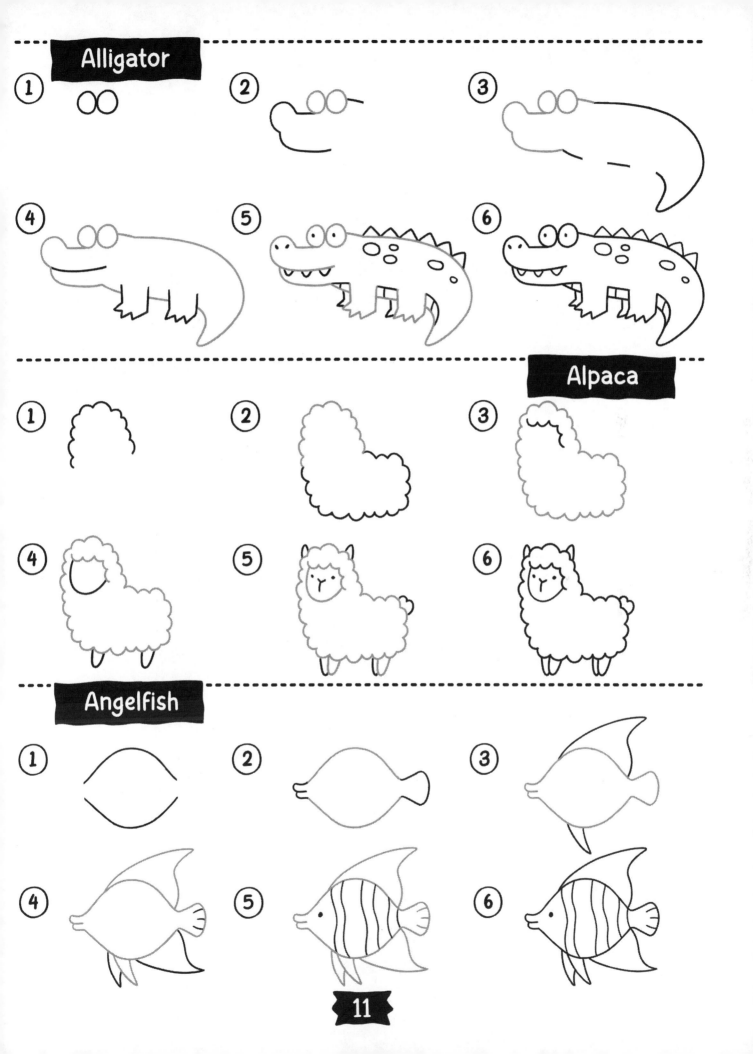

Alligator

① ② ③

④ ⑤ ⑥

Alpaca

① ② ③

④ ⑤ ⑥

Angelfish

① ② ③

④ ⑤ ⑥

11

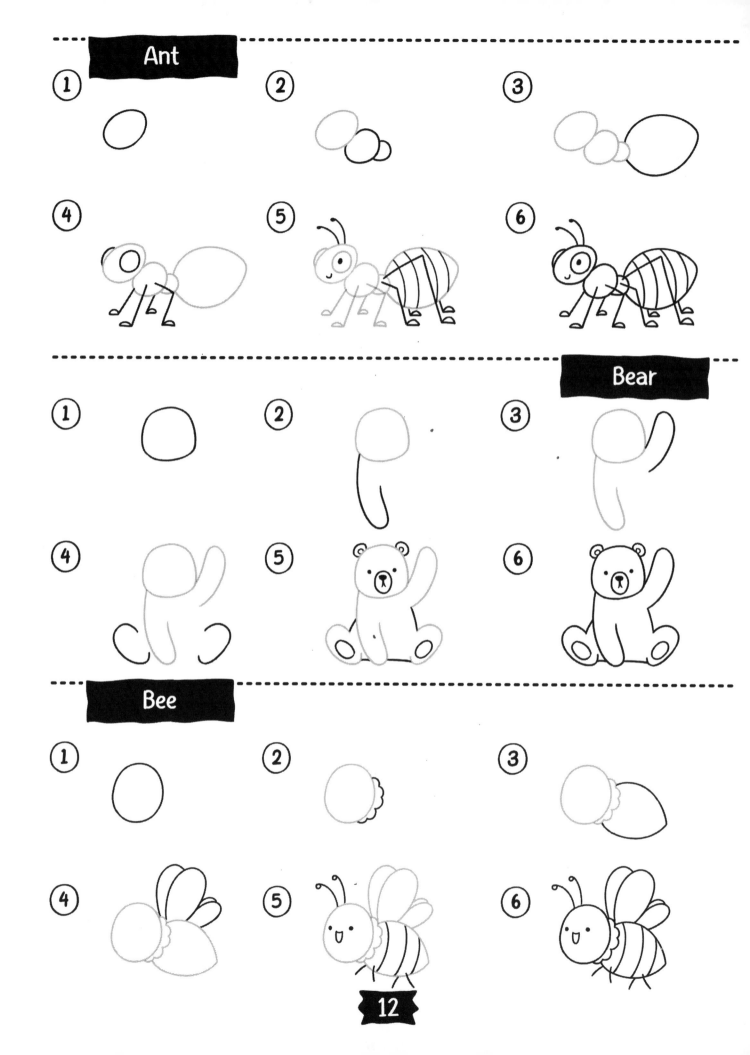

Ant

Bear

Bee

12

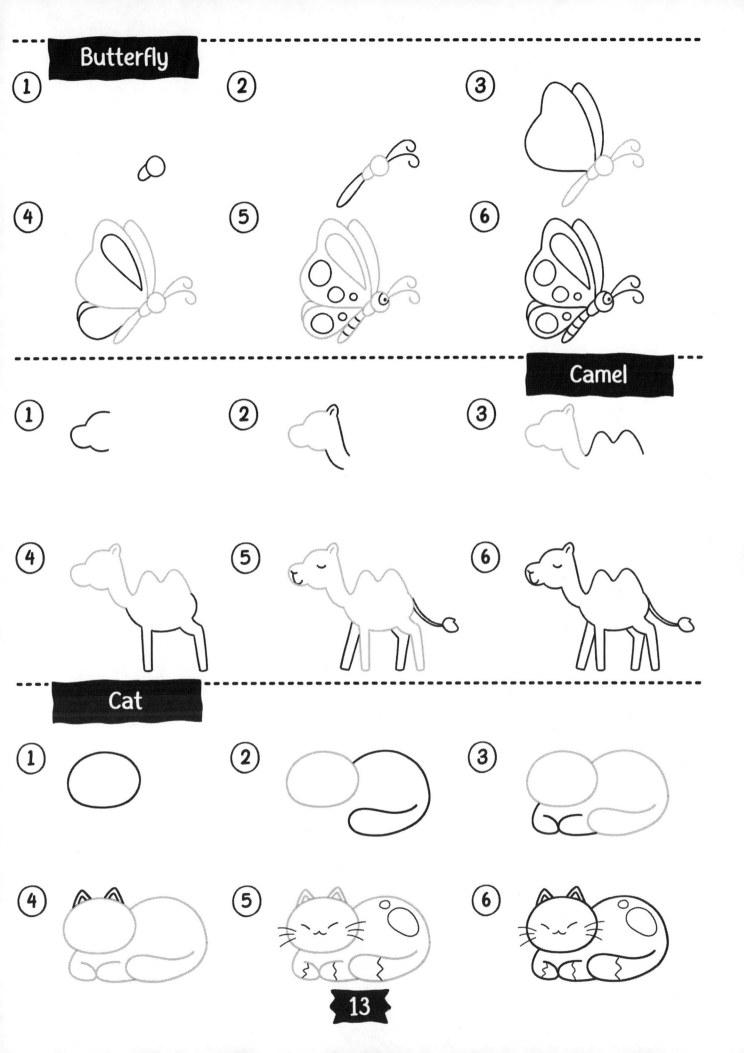

Butterfly

Camel

Cat

13

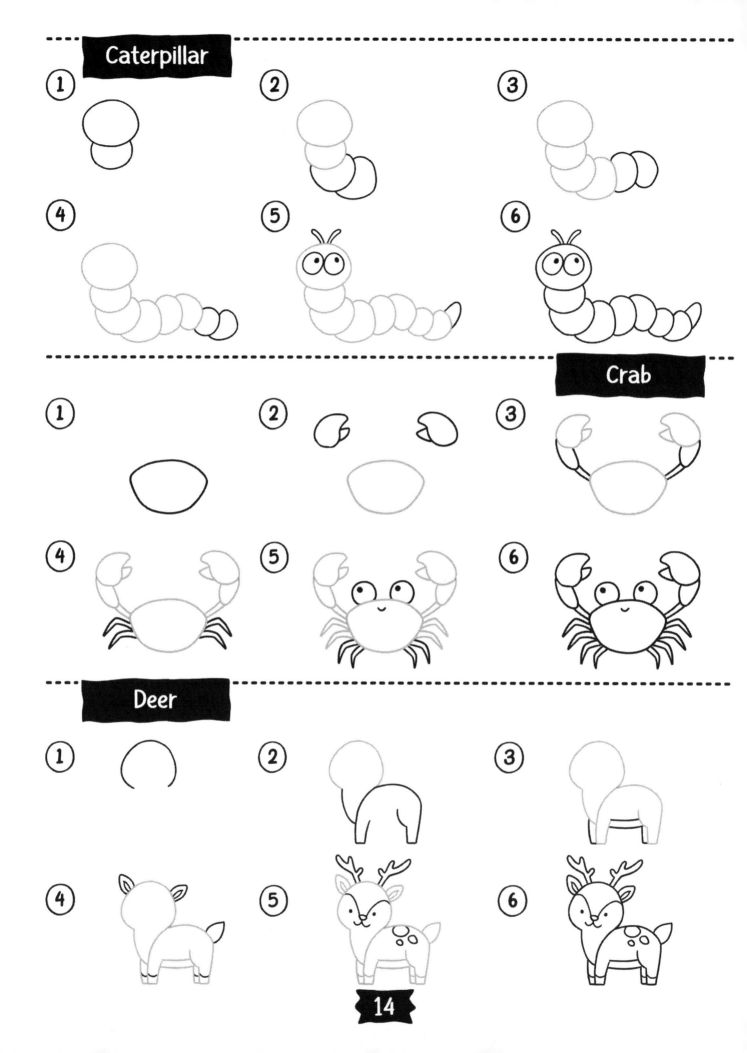

Caterpillar

Crab

Deer

14

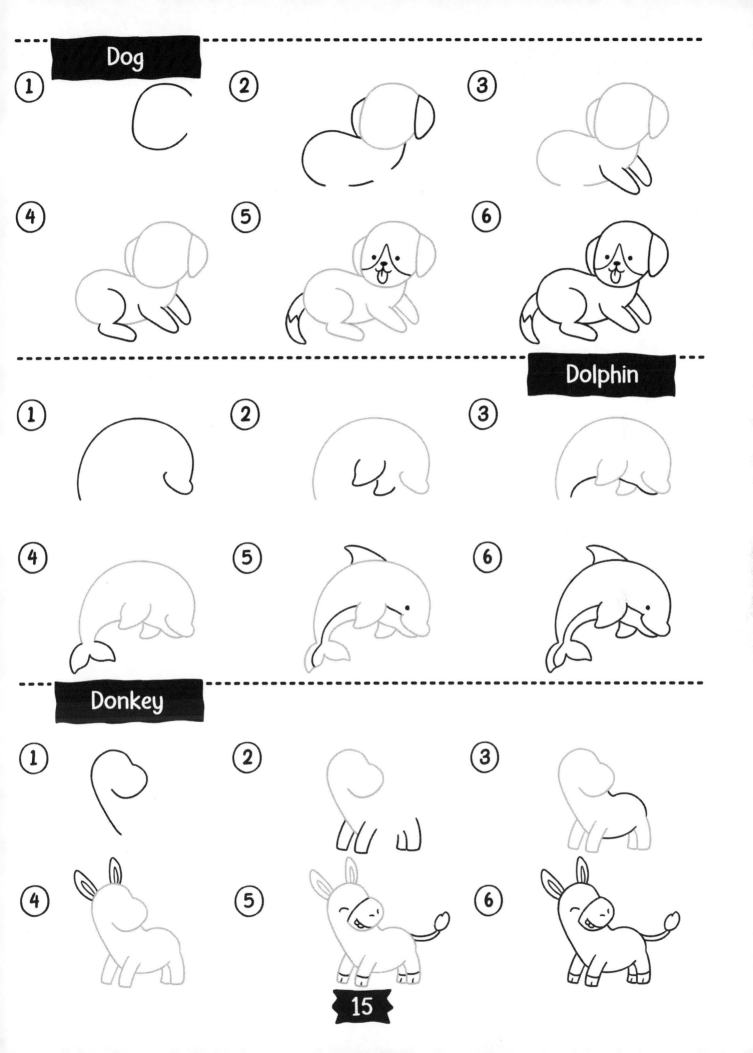

Dog

① ② ③
④ ⑤ ⑥

Dolphin

① ② ③
④ ⑤ ⑥

Donkey

① ② ③
④ ⑤ ⑥

15

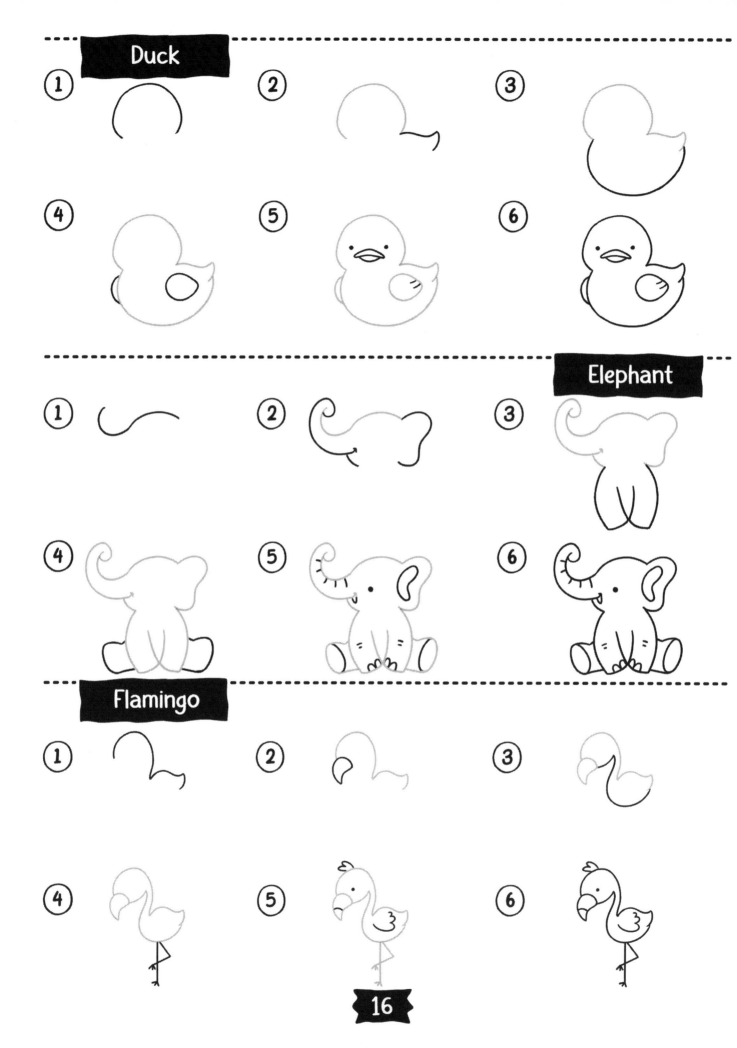

Duck

Elephant

Flamingo

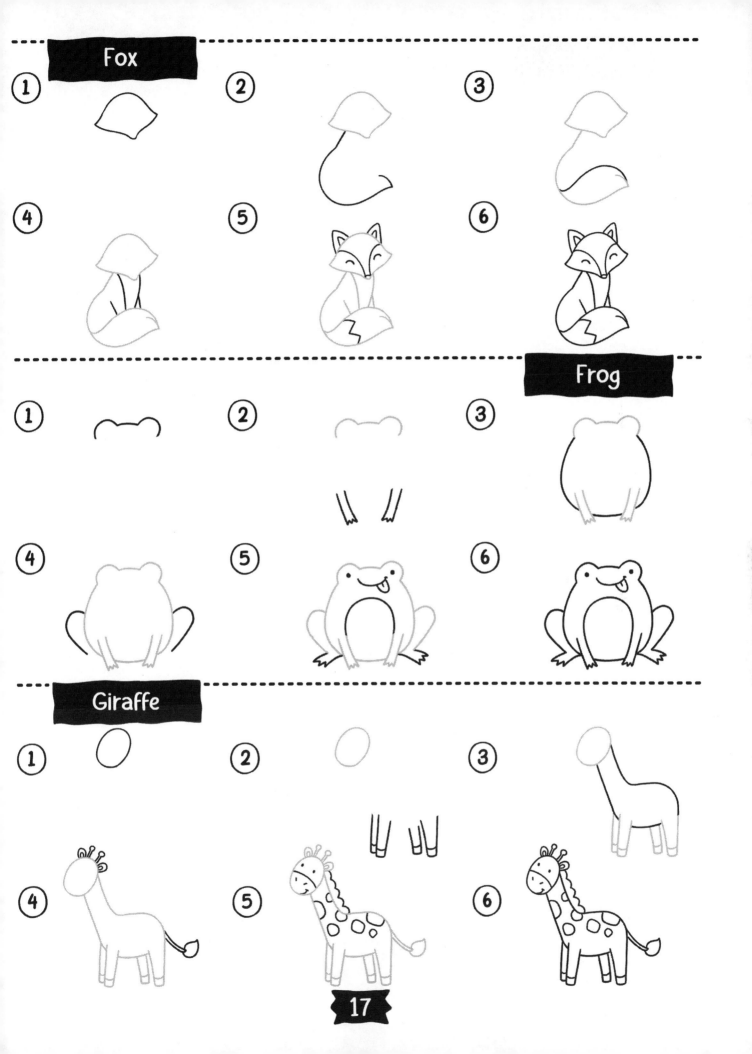

Fox

Frog

Giraffe

17

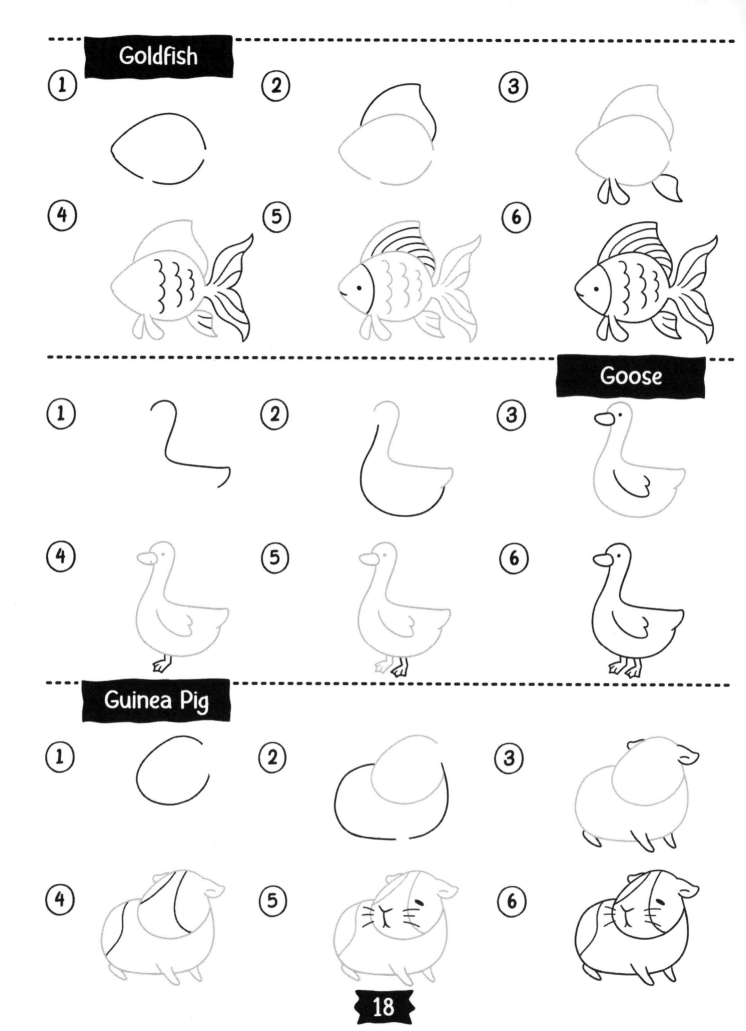

Goldfish

Goose

Guinea Pig

18

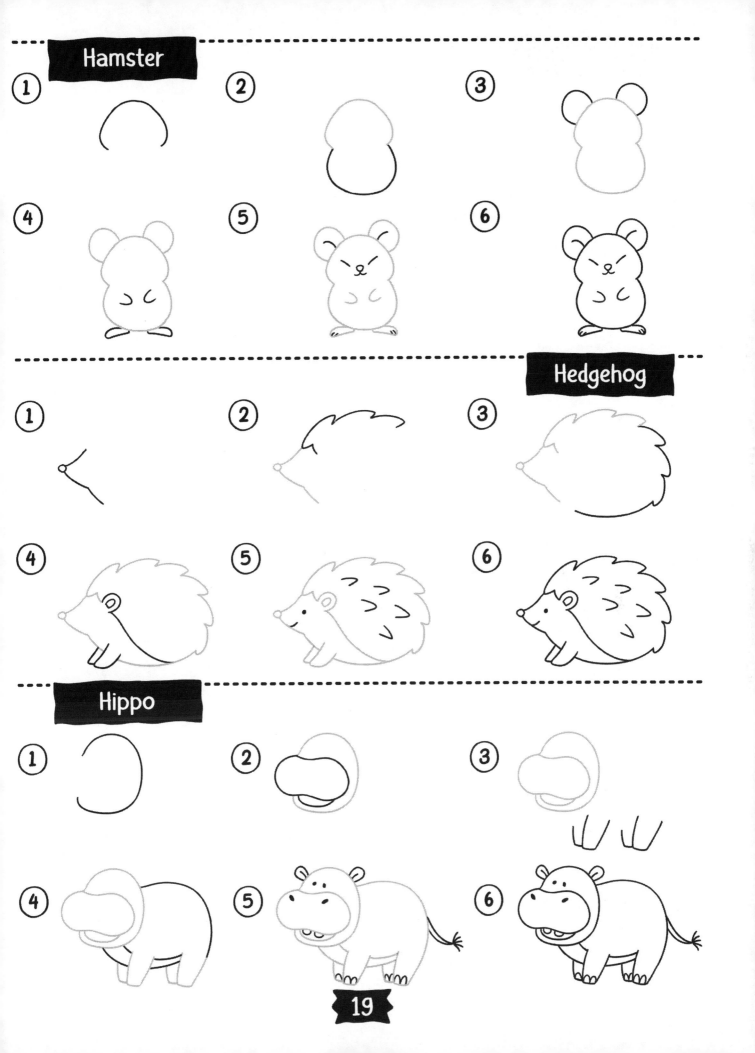

Hamster

1 2 3
4 5 6

Hedgehog

1 2 3
4 5 6

Hippo

1 2 3
4 5 6

Horse

Jellyfish

Kangaroo

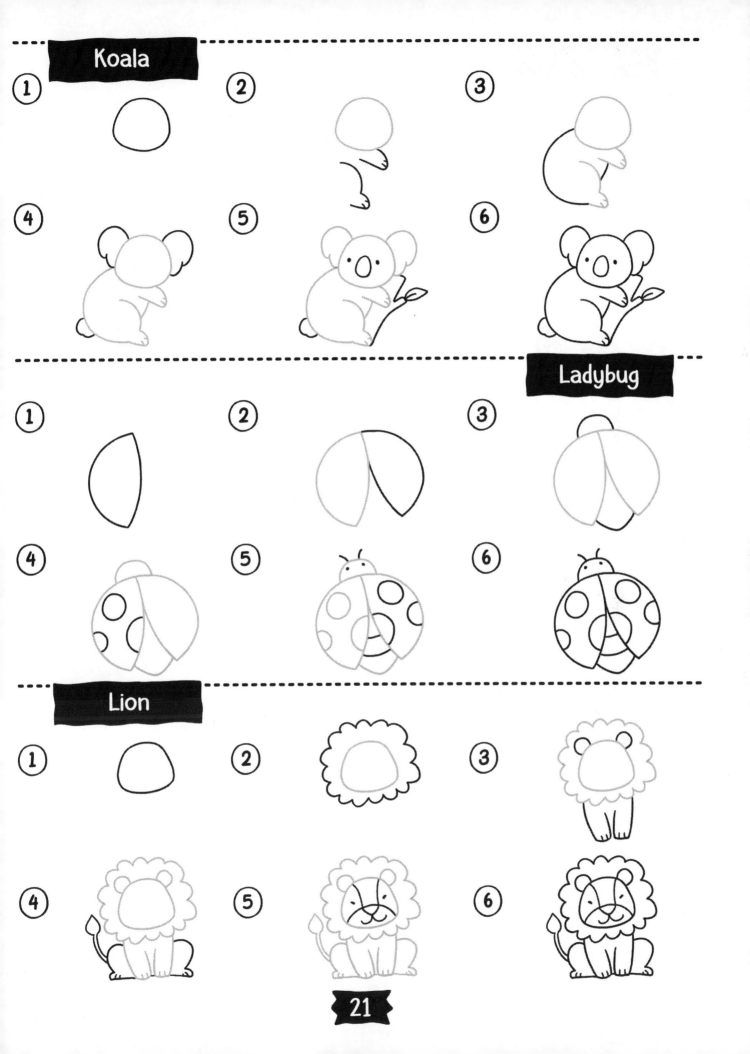

Koala

① ② ③
④ ⑤ ⑥

Ladybug

① ② ③
④ ⑤ ⑥

Lion

① ② ③
④ ⑤ ⑥

21

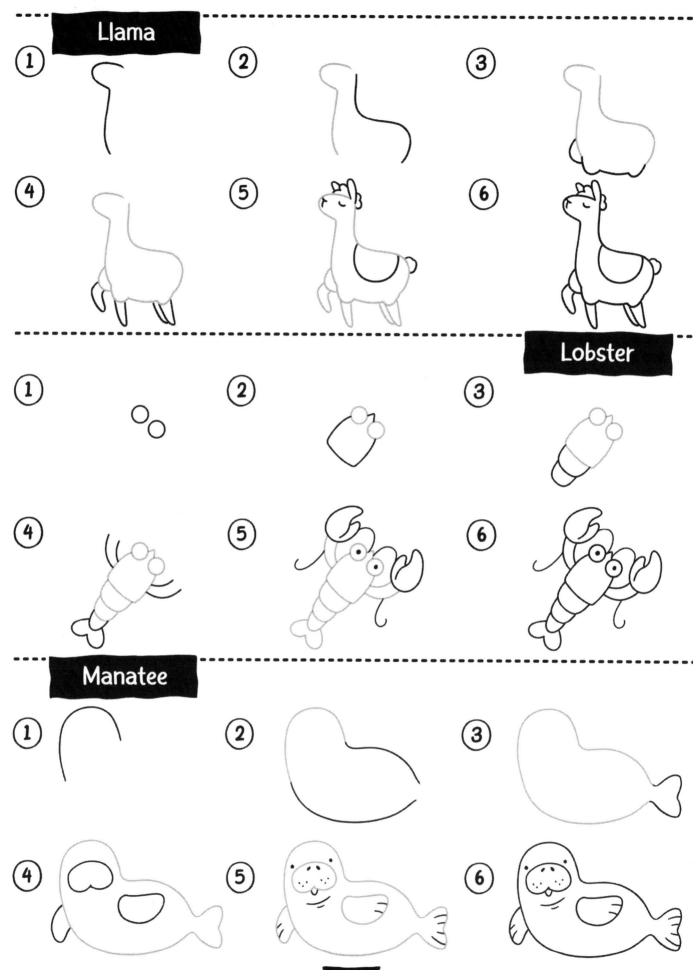

Llama

Lobster

Manatee

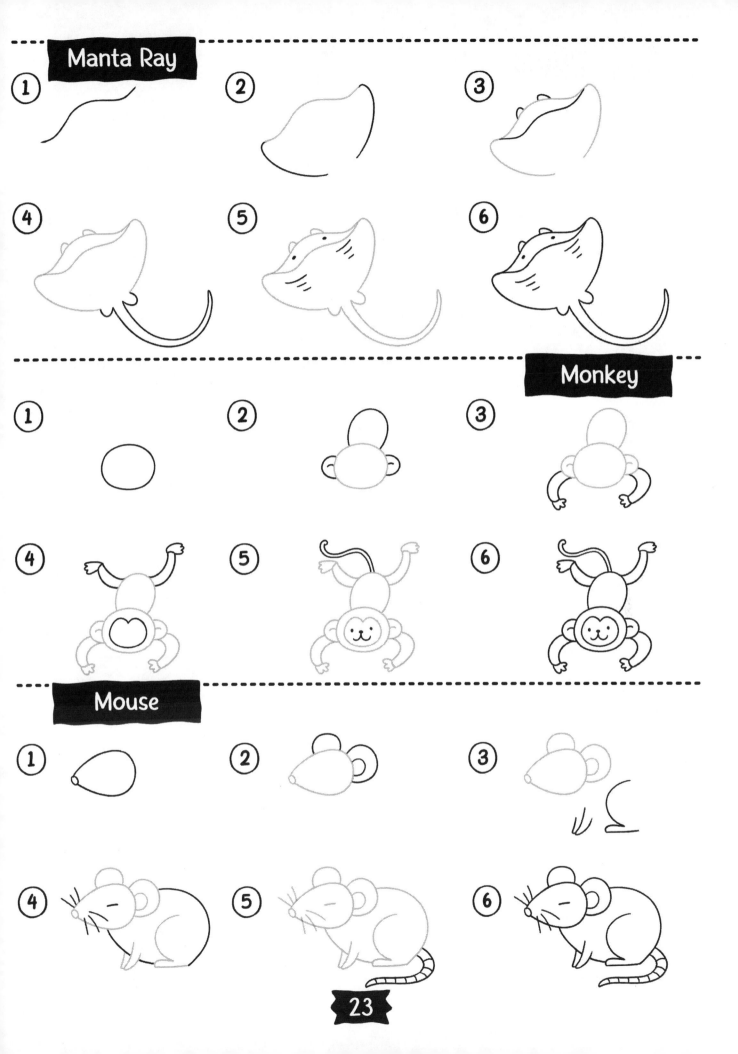

Manta Ray

1 2 3

4 5 6

Monkey

1 2 3

4 5 6

Mouse

1 2 3

4 5 6

23

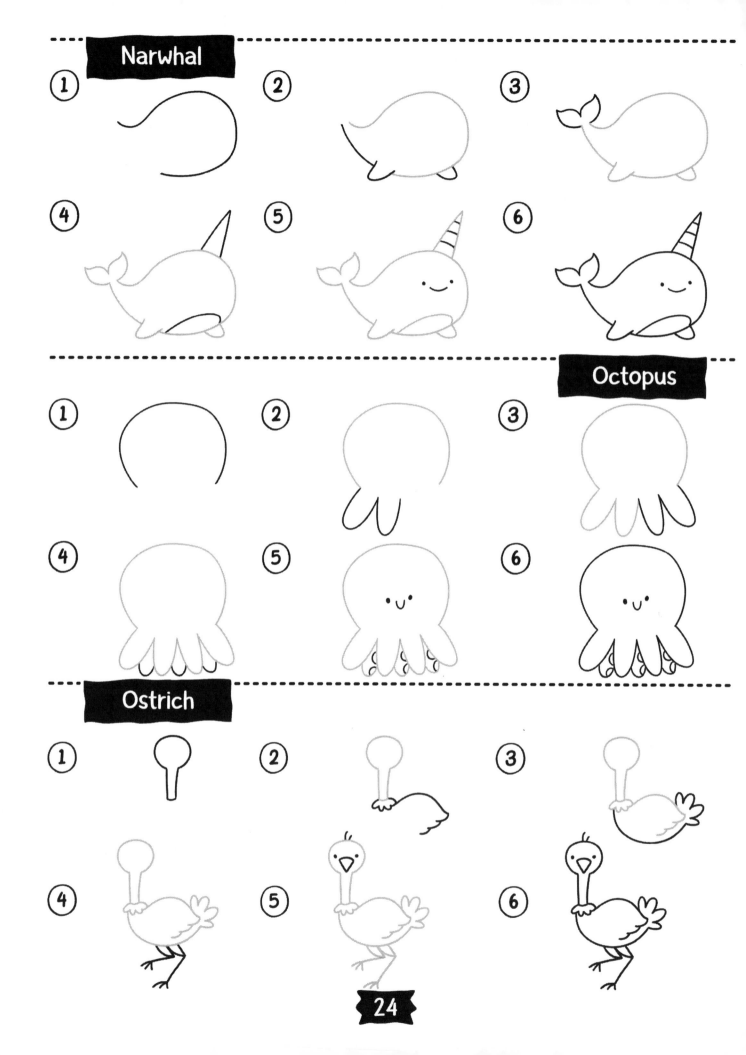

Narwhal

Octopus

Ostrich

24

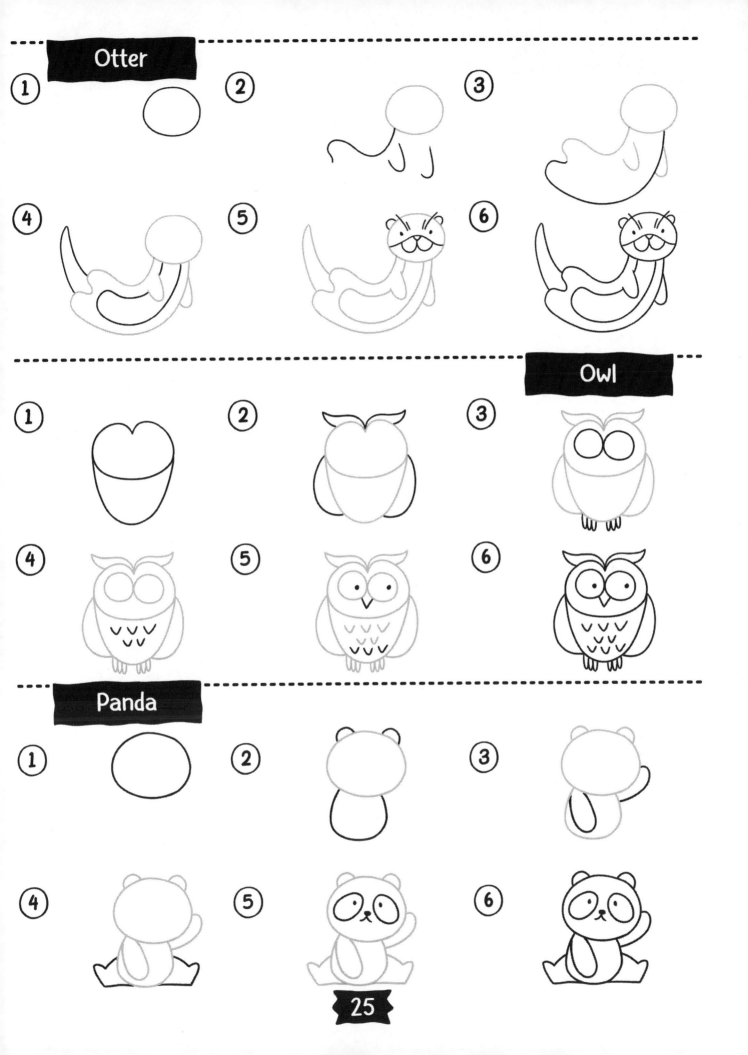

Otter

① ② ③
④ ⑤ ⑥

Owl

① ② ③
④ ⑤ ⑥

Panda

① ② ③
④ ⑤ ⑥

25

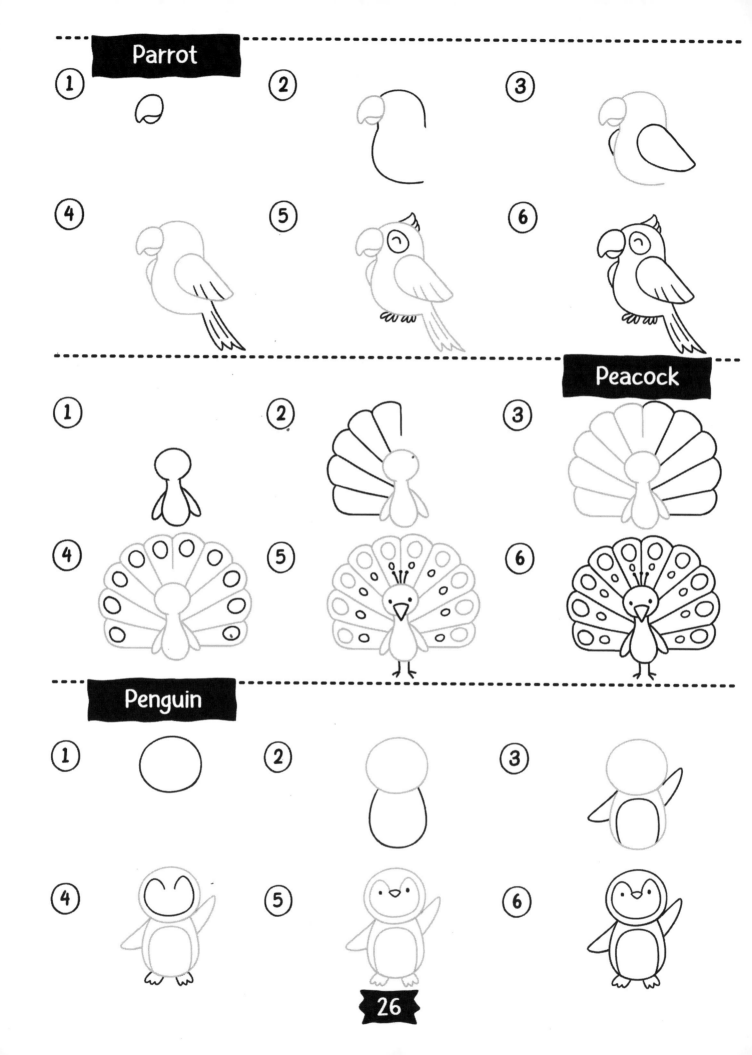

Parrot

① ② ③

④ ⑤ ⑥

Peacock

① ② ③

④ ⑤ ⑥

Penguin

① ② ③

④ ⑤ ⑥

26

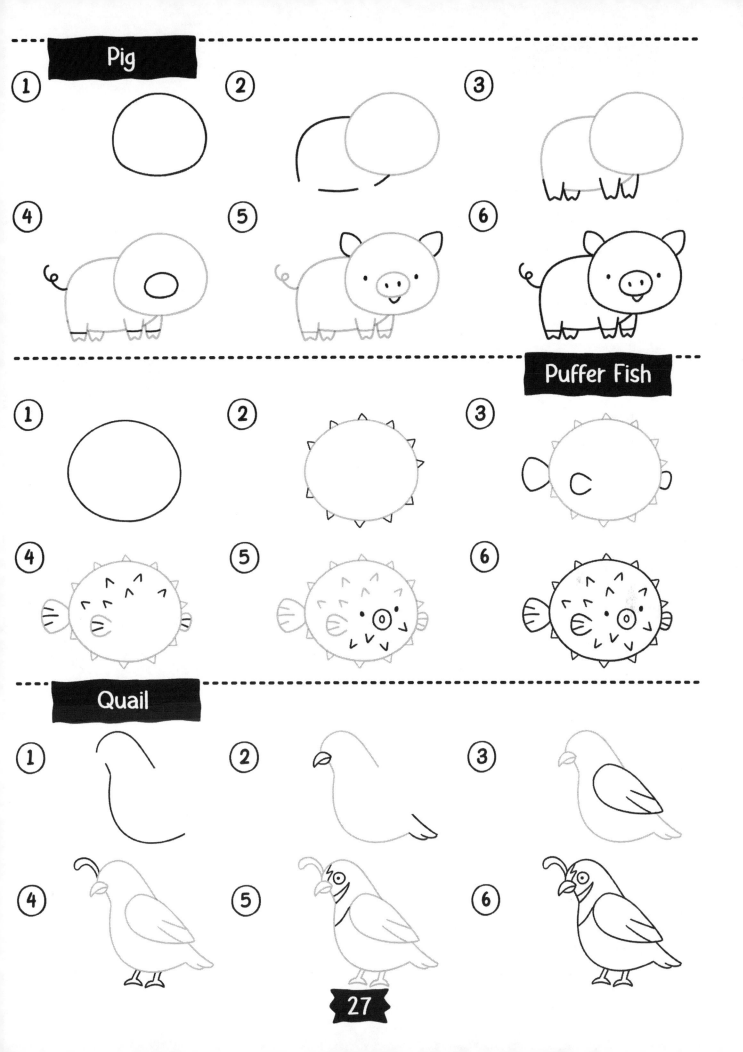

Pig

Puffer Fish

Quail

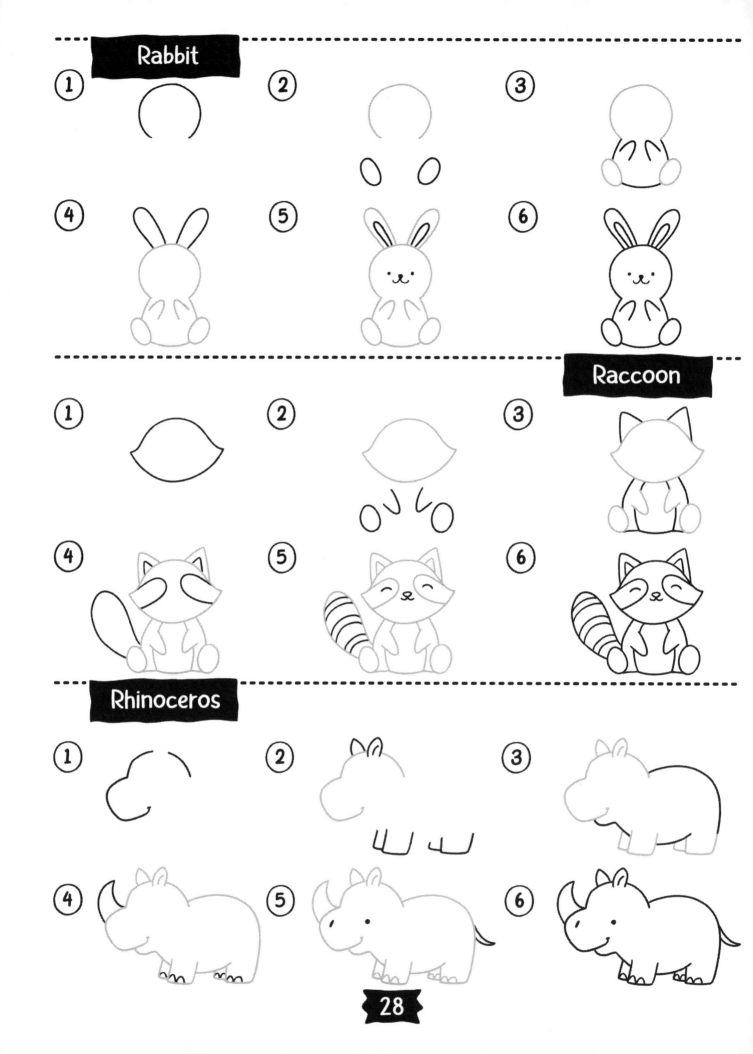

Rabbit

Raccoon

Rhinoceros

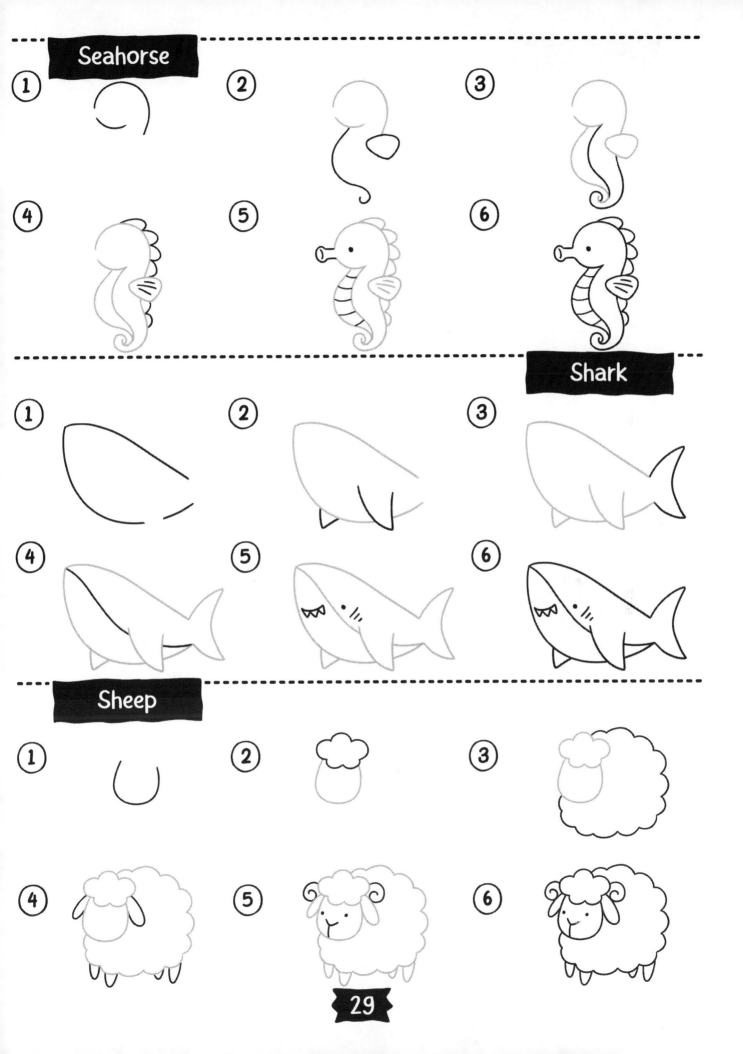

Seahorse

Shark

Sheep

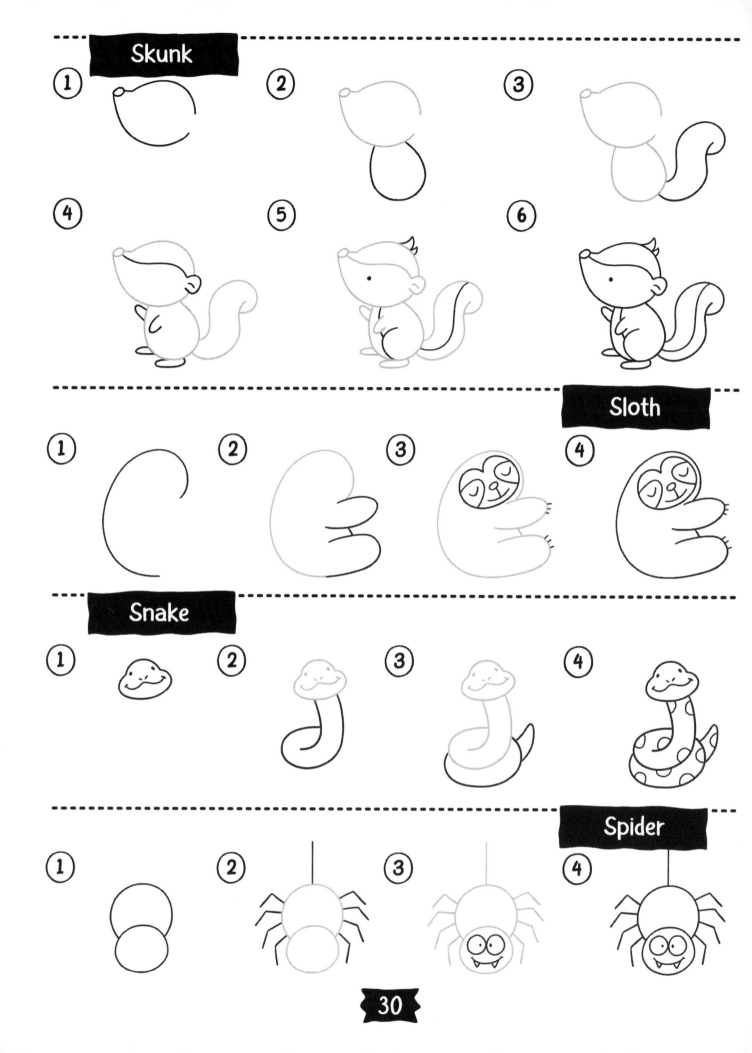

Skunk

Sloth

Snake

Spider

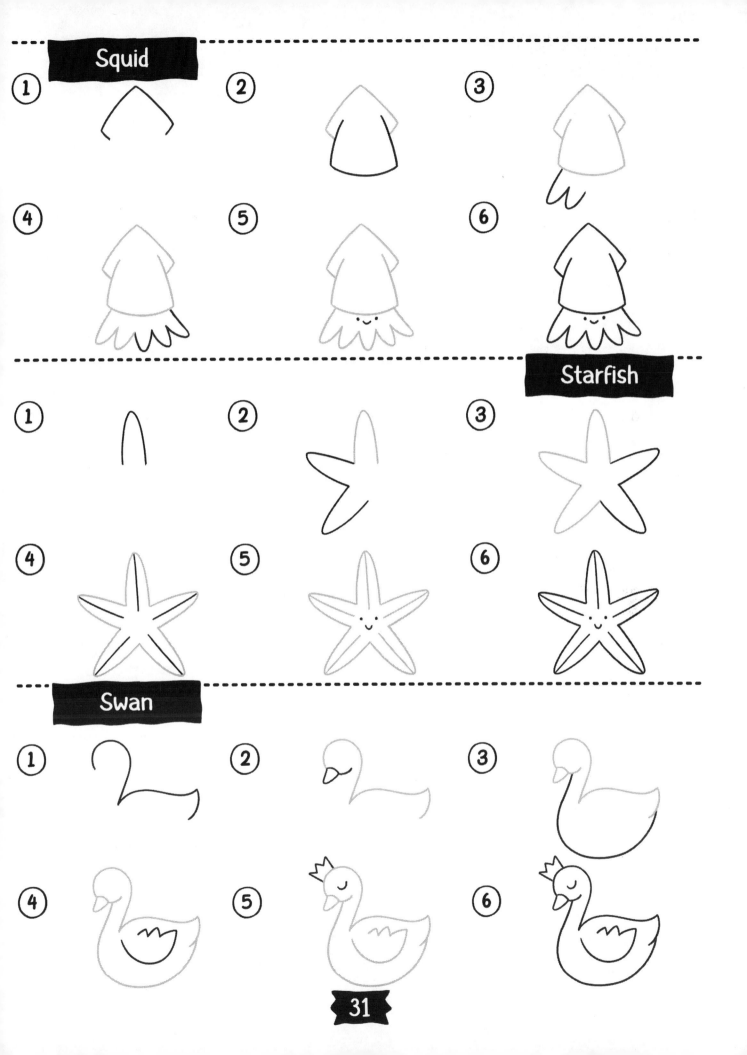

Squid

Starfish

Swan

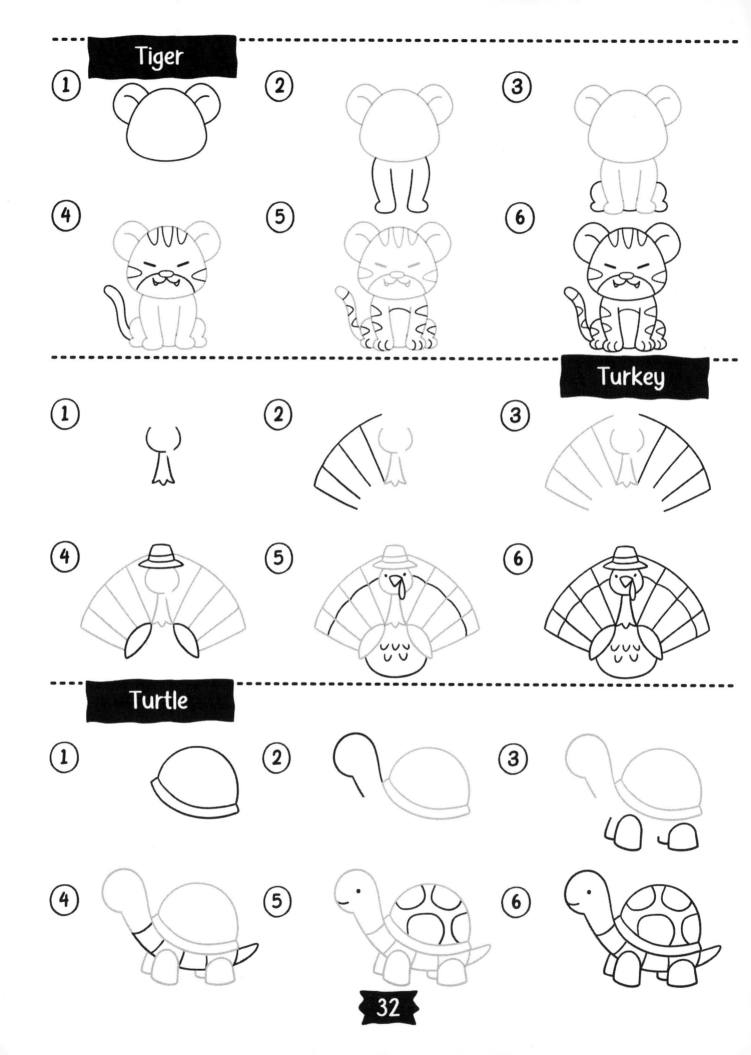

Tiger

Turkey

Turtle

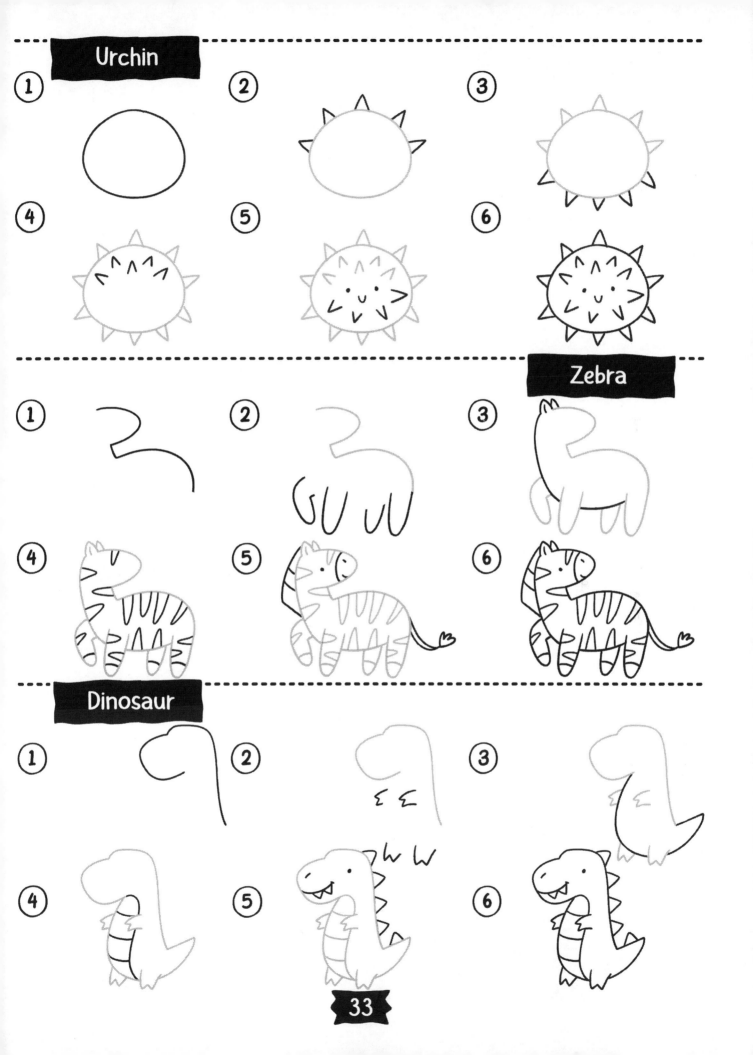

Urchin

① ② ③
④ ⑤ ⑥

Zebra

① ② ③
④ ⑤ ⑥

Dinosaur

① ② ③
④ ⑤ ⑥

1
2
3
4

1
2
3
4

1
2
3
4

1
2
3
4

1
2
3
4

Banana

① ② ③ ④

Bell Pepper

① ② ③ ④

Blueberries

① ② ③ ④

Bread

① ② ③ ④

Broccoli

① ② ③ ④

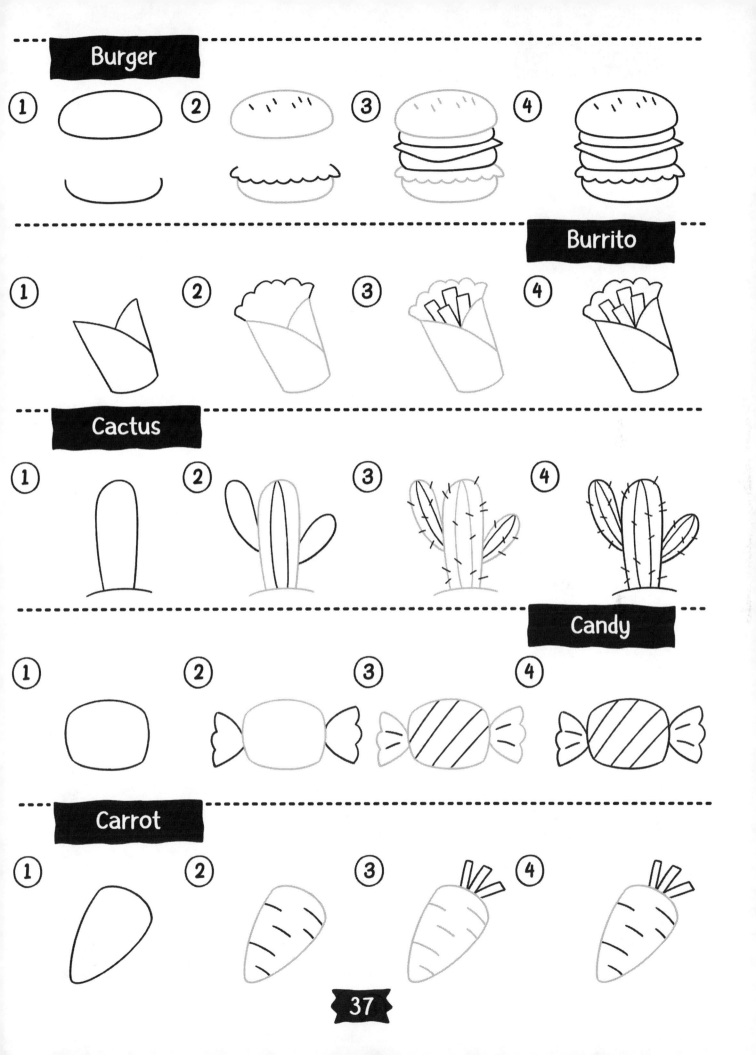

Burger

① ② ③ ④

Burrito

① ② ③ ④

Cactus

① ② ③ ④

Candy

① ② ③ ④

Carrot

① ② ③ ④

37

Cheese

① ② ③ ④

Cheese Cake

① ② ③ ④

Cherries

① ② ③ ④

Chili Pepper

① ② ③ ④

Chips

① ② ③ ④

Chocolate Bar

① ② ③ ④

Clover

① ② ③ ④

Coconut

① ② ③ ④

Cookies

① ② ③ ④

Corn

① ② ③ ④

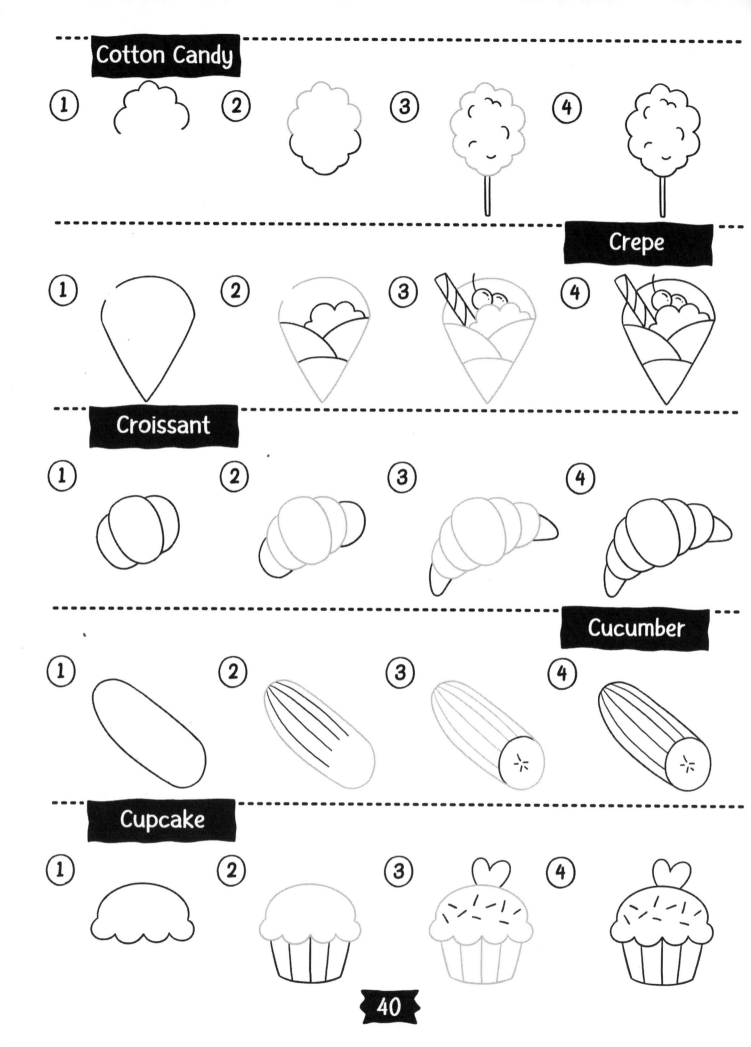

Cotton Candy

1 2 3 4

Crepe

1 2 3 4

Croissant

1 2 3 4

Cucumber

1 2 3 4

Cupcake

1 2 3 4

Dandelion

① ② ③ ④

Donut

① ② ③ ④

Dragonfruit

① ② ③ ④

Durian

① ② ③ ④

Egg Plant

① ② ③ ④

French Fries

1
2
3
4

French Toast

1
2
3
4

Fried Egg

1
2
3
4

Grape

1
2
3
4

Honey

1
2
3
4

Hot Chocolate

① ② ③

④ ⑤ ⑥

Hot Dog

① ② ③ ④

Ice Cream

① ② ③ ④

Jackfruit

① ② ③ ④

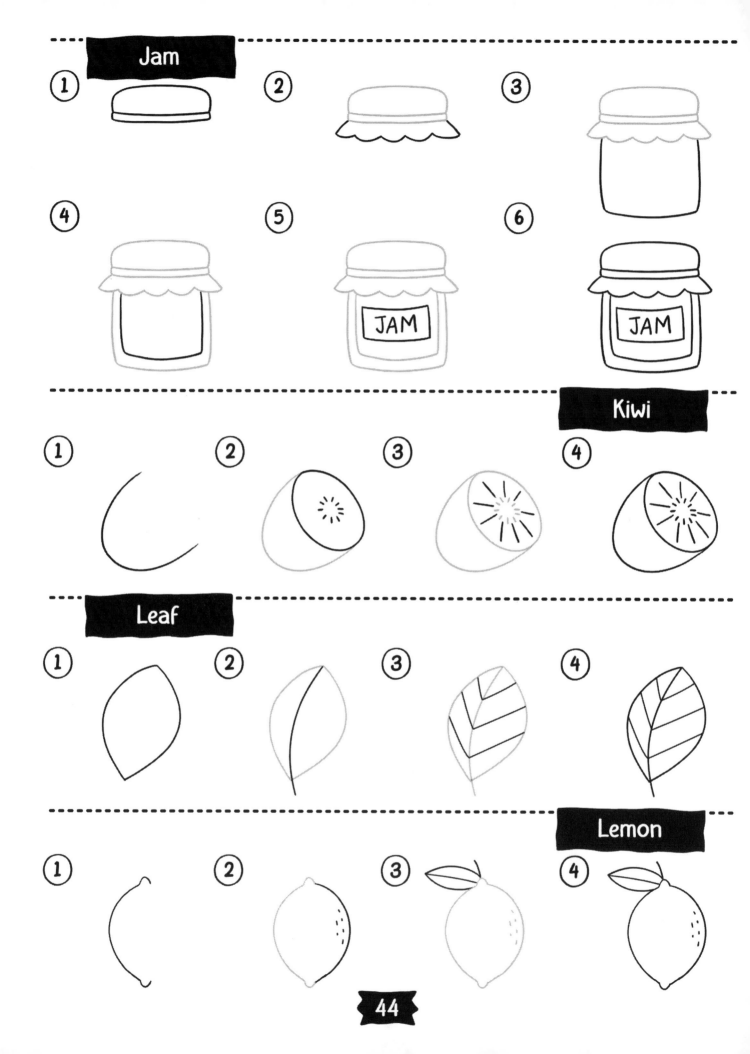

Jam

① ② ③

④ ⑤ JAM ⑥ JAM

Kiwi

① ② ③ ④

Leaf

① ② ③ ④

Lemon

① ② ③ ④

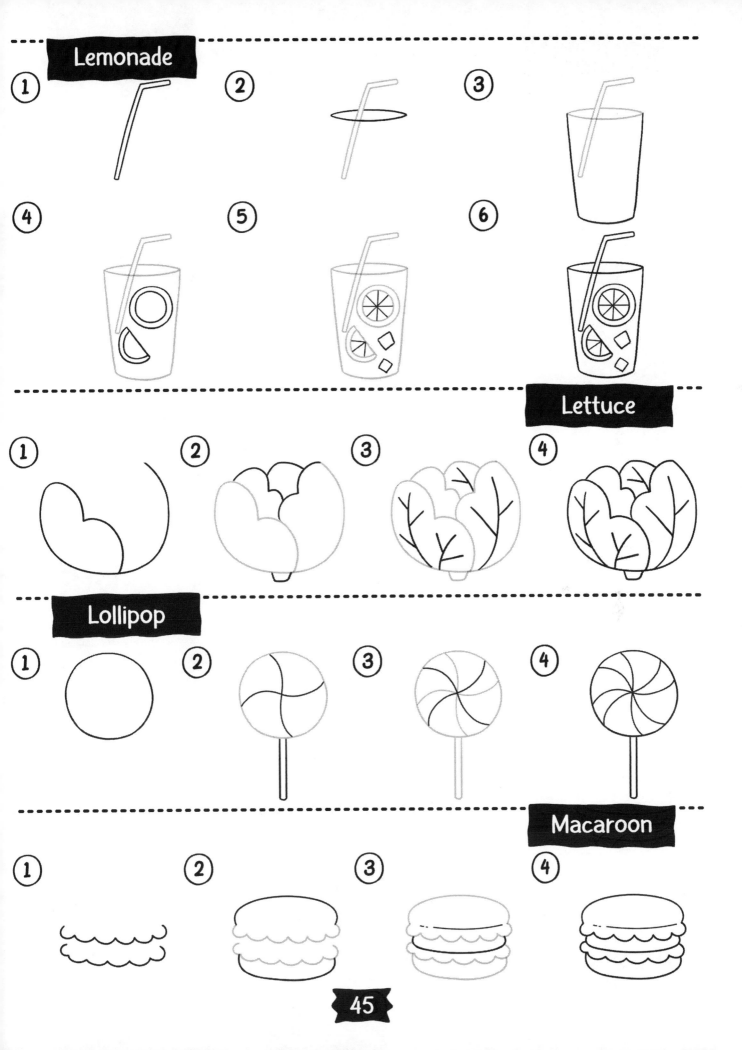

Lemonade

1
2
3
4
5
6

Lettuce

1
2
3
4

Lollipop

1
2
3
4

Macaroon

1
2
3
4

45

① ② ③ ④

Mangosteen

① ② ③ ④

Marshmallow

① ② ③ ④

Milkshake

① ② ③

④ ⑤ ⑥

Muffin

① ② ③ ④

Mushroom

① ② ③ ④

Noodles

① ② ③

④ ⑤ ⑥

Onion

① ② ③ ④

① ② ③ ④

① ② ③ ④

① ② ③

④ ⑤ ⑥

① ② ③ ④

Panna Cotta

① ② ③ ④

Papaya

① ② ③ ④

Passion Fruit

① ② ③

④ ⑤ ⑥

Peach

① ② ③ ④

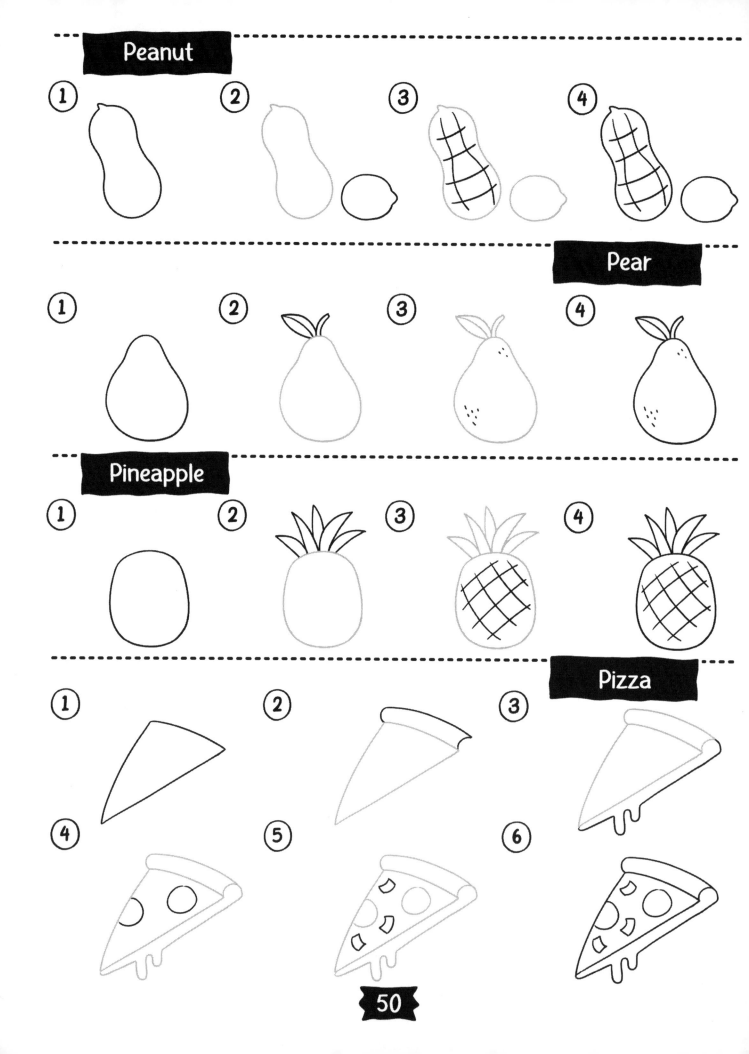

Peanut

① ② ③ ④

Pear

① ② ③ ④

Pineapple

① ② ③ ④

Pizza

① ② ③
④ ⑤ ⑥

50

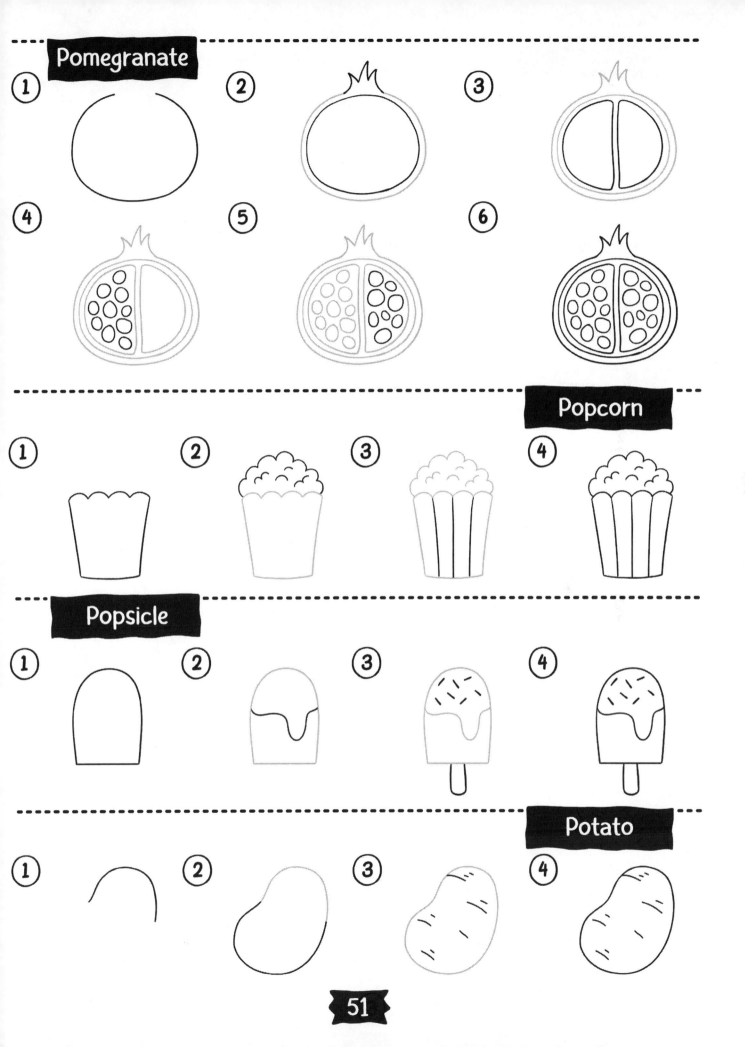

Pomegranate

① ② ③
④ ⑤ ⑥

Popcorn

① ② ③ ④

Popsicle

① ② ③ ④

Potato

① ② ③ ④

Pretzel

① ② ③ ④

Pudding

① ② ③

④ ⑤ ⑥

Pumpkin

① ② ③ ④

Rambutan

① ② ③ ④

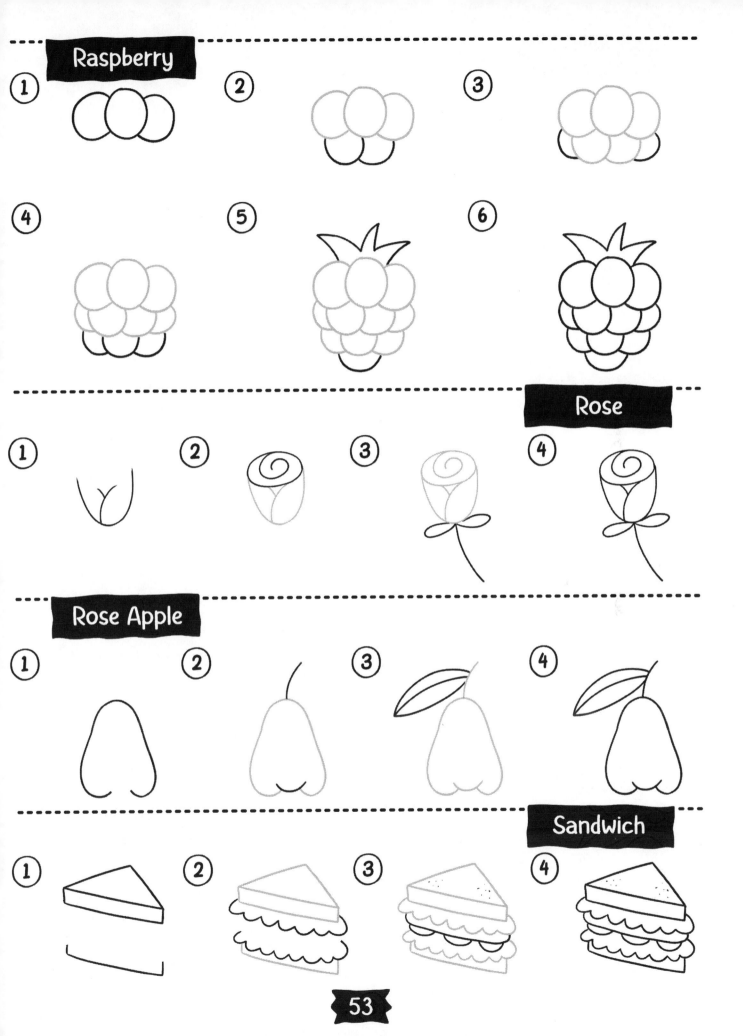

Raspberry

Rose

Rose Apple

Sandwich

53

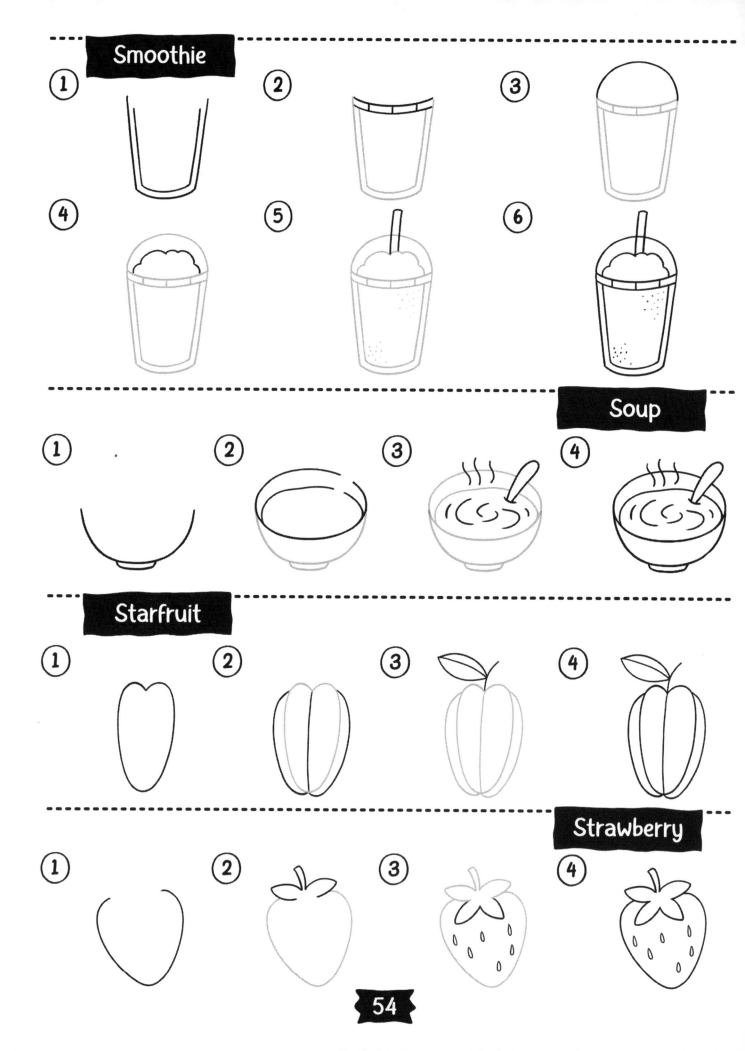

Smoothie

① ② ③

④ ⑤ ⑥

Soup

① ② ③ ④

Starfruit

① ② ③ ④

Strawberry

① ② ③ ④

1 2 3 4

Sunflower

1 2 3

4 5 6

Sushi

1 2 3 4

Tacos

1 2 3 4

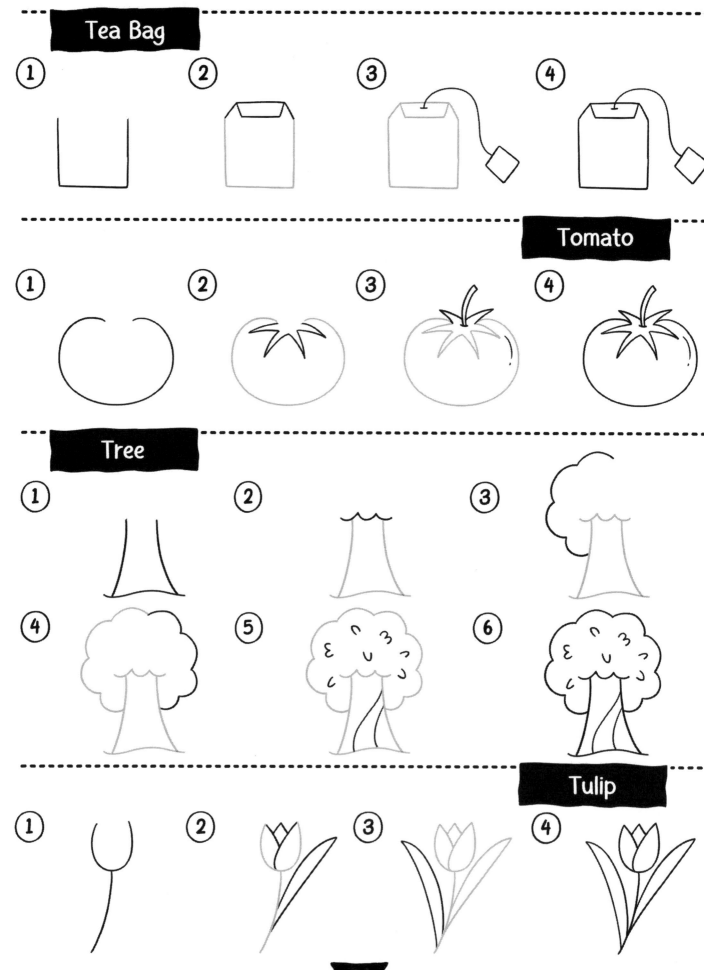

Tea Bag

① ② ③ ④

Tomato

① ② ③ ④

Tree

① ② ③

④ ⑤ ⑥

Tulip

① ② ③ ④

56

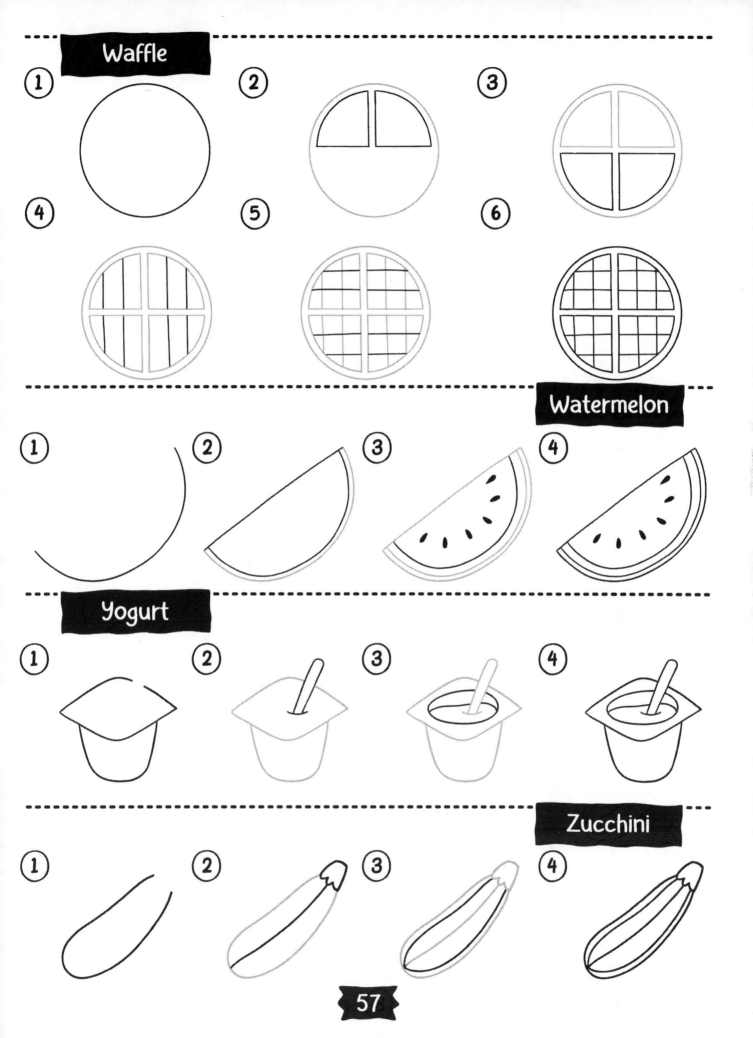

Waffle

① ② ③
④ ⑤ ⑥

Watermelon

① ② ③ ④

Yogurt

① ② ③ ④

Zucchini

① ② ③ ④

Toys, Vehicles & Outer Space

Badminton Racket

① ② ③ ④

Balloon

① ② ③ ④

Baseball Bat

① ② ③ ④

Baseball Gloves

① ② ③ ④

Basket Ball

① ② ③ ④

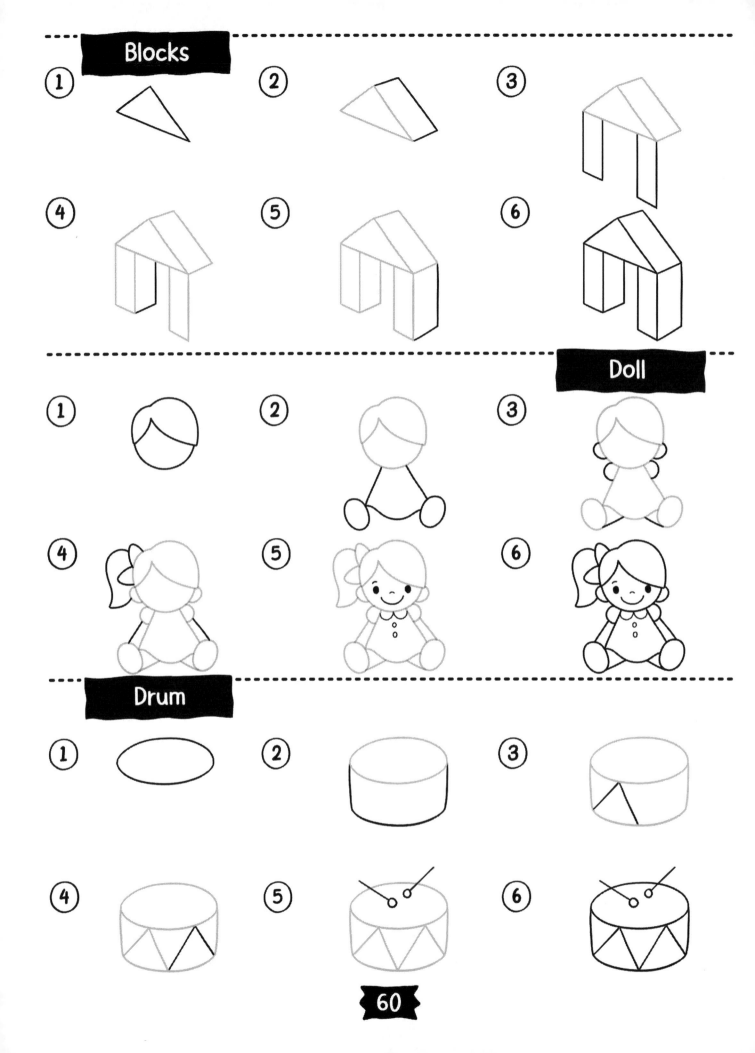

Blocks

① ② ③
④ ⑤ ⑥

Doll

① ② ③
④ ⑤ ⑥

Drum

① ② ③
④ ⑤ ⑥

60

Guitar

1. 2. 3. 4.

Kite

1. 2. 3. 4.

Maracas

1. 2. 3.

4. 5. 6.

Pinwheel

1. 2. 3. 4.

61

Robot

① ② ③ ④

Rubber Duck

① ② ③ ④

Shuttlecock

① ② ③ ④

Skateboard

① ② ③ ④

Soccer Ball

① ② ③ ④

Spinning Top

① ② ③ ④

Teddy Bear

① ② ③ ④

Tennis Ball

① ② ③ ④

Xylophone

① ② ③ ④

Yo Yo

① ② ③ ④

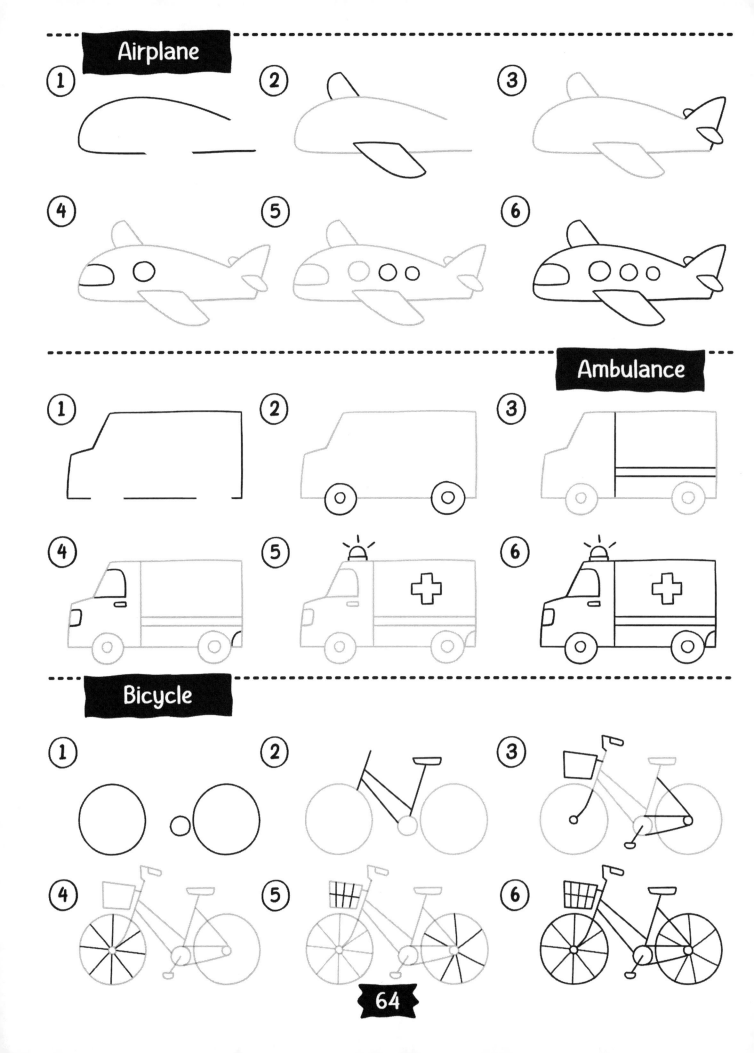

Airplane

Ambulance

Bicycle

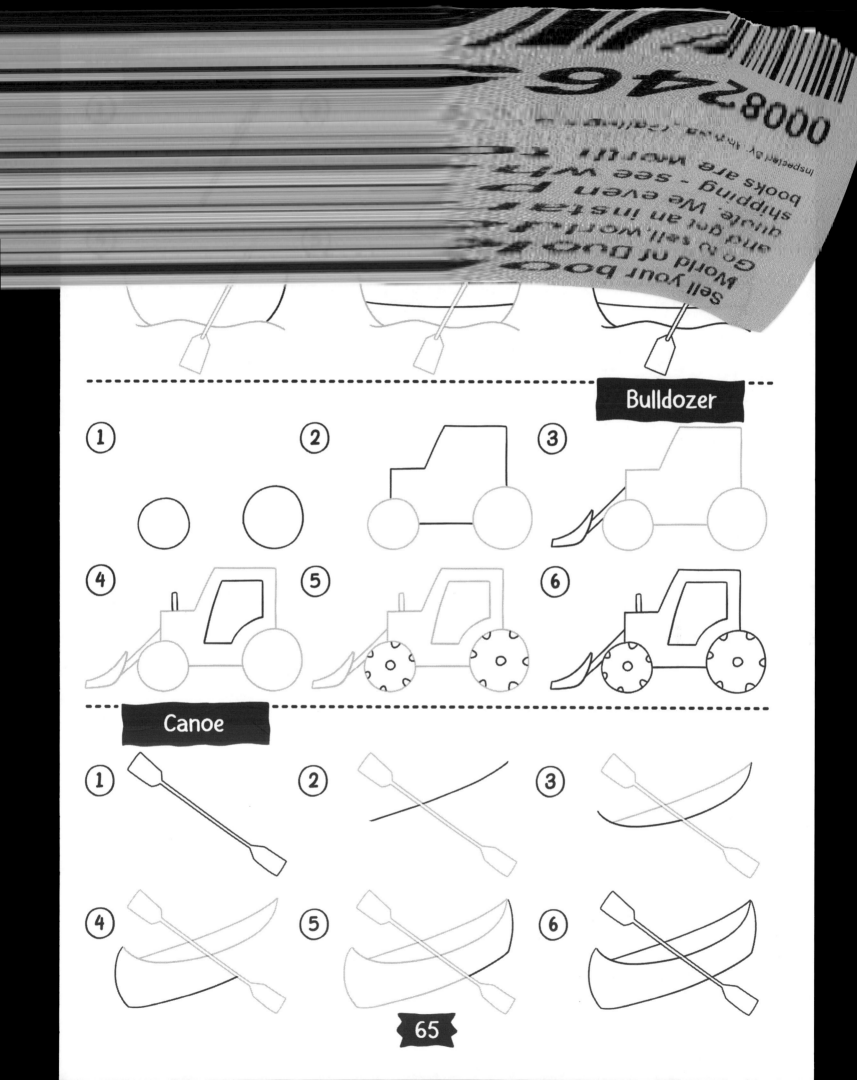

Bulldozer

① ② ③
④ ⑤ ⑥

Canoe

① ② ③
④ ⑤ ⑥

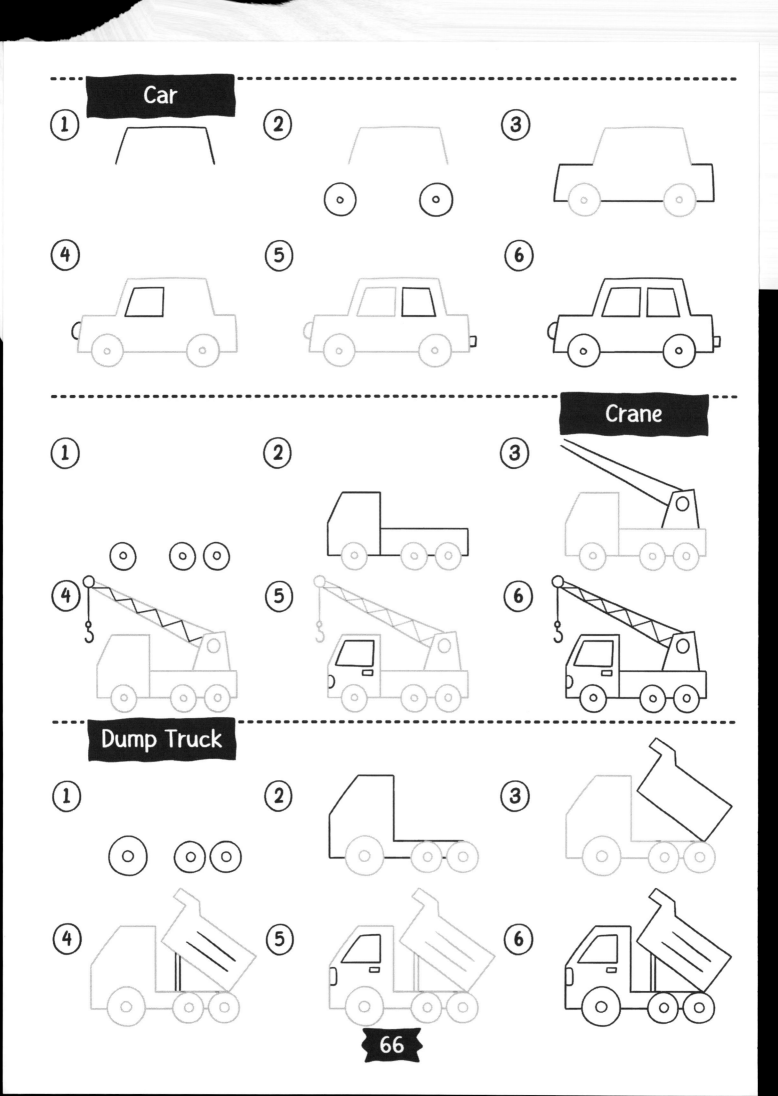

Car

① ② ③

④ ⑤ ⑥

Crane

① ② ③

④ ⑤ ⑥

Dump Truck

① ② ③

④ ⑤ ⑥

Excavator

①

②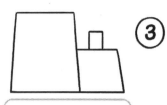

③

④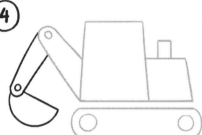

⑤

⑥

Fire Truck

①

②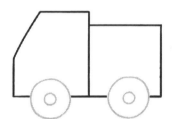

③

④

⑤

⑥

Helicopter

①

②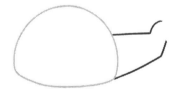

③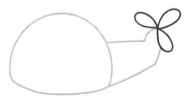

④

⑤

⑥

Hot Air Balloon

① ② ③

④ ⑤ ⑥

Motor Boat

① ② ③

④ ⑤ ⑥

Pickup Truck

① ② ③

④ ⑤ ⑥

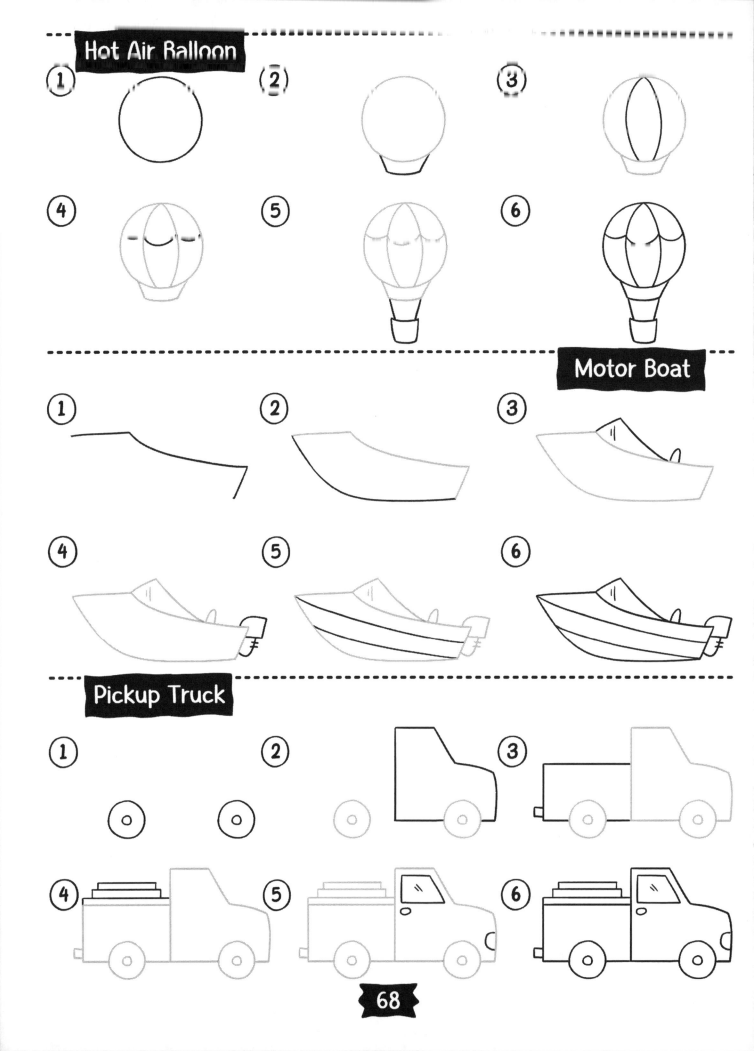

68

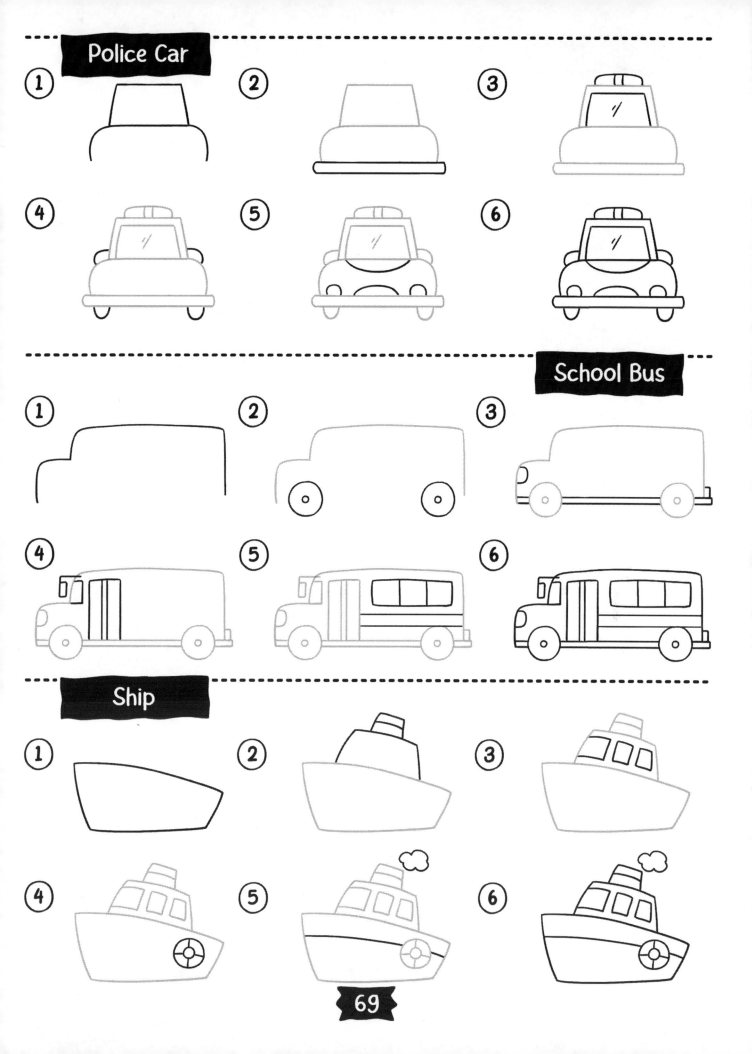

Police Car

School Bus

Ship

69

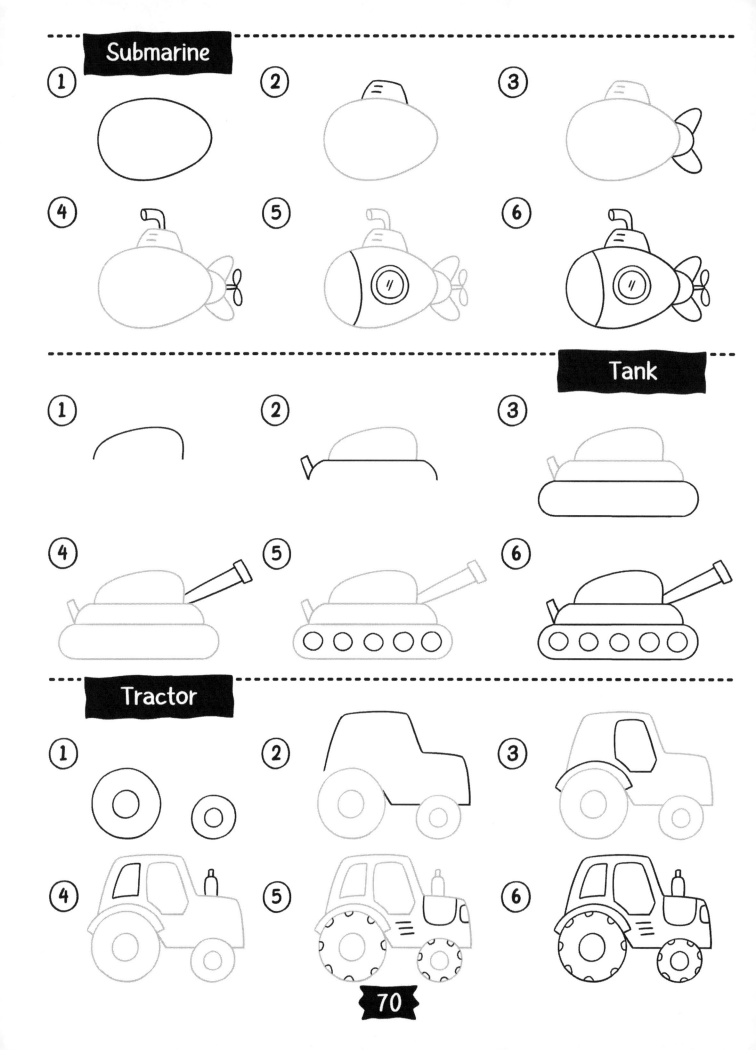

Submarine

Tank

Tractor

70

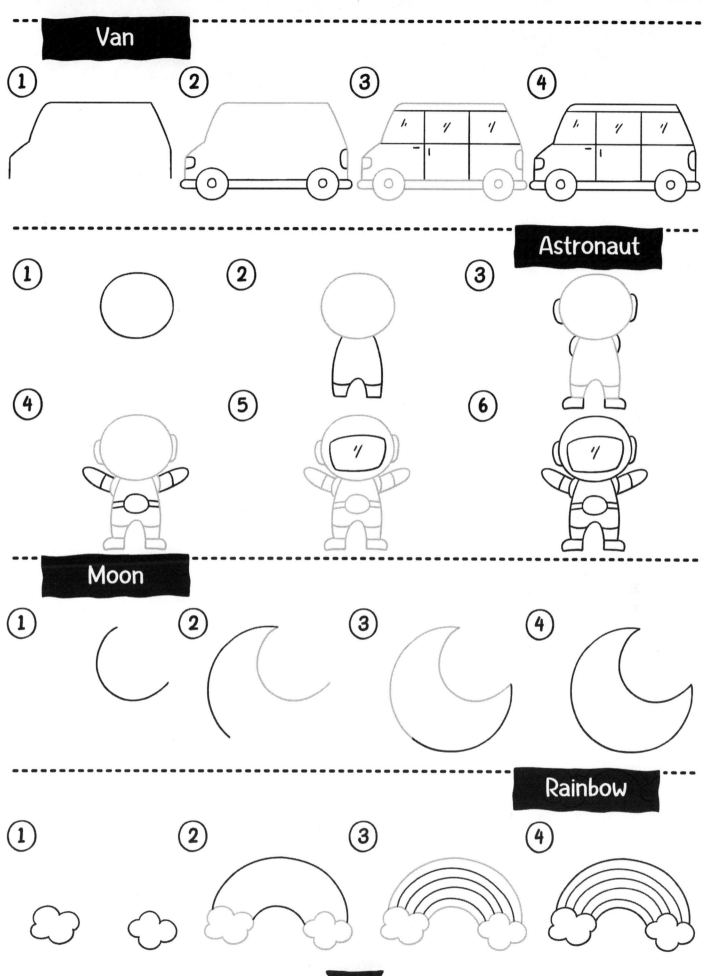

Van

Astronaut

Moon

Rainbow

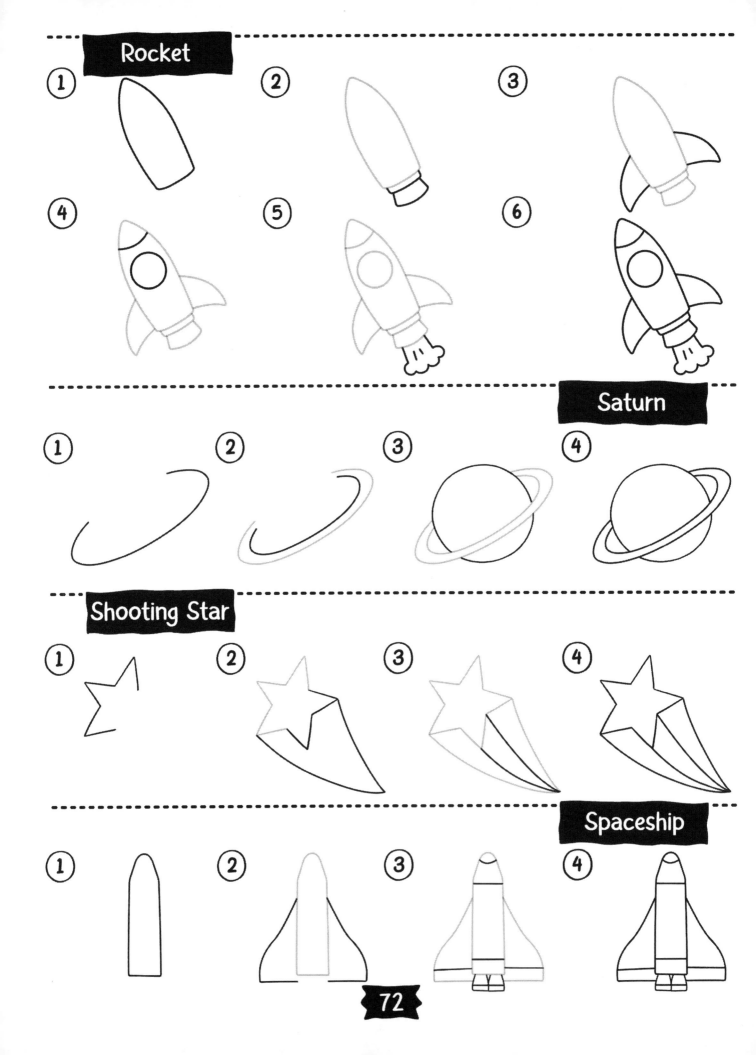

Rocket

① ② ③

④ ⑤ ⑥

Saturn

① ② ③ ④

Shooting Star

① ② ③ ④

Spaceship

① ② ③ ④

Star

1
2
3
4

Sun

1
2
3
4

Telescope

1
2
3
4
5
6

UFO

1
2
3
4

Celebration

Bell

① ② ③ ④

Chick

① ② ③ ④

Easter Basket

① ② ③
④ ⑤ ⑥

Easter Bonnet

① ② ③ ④

75

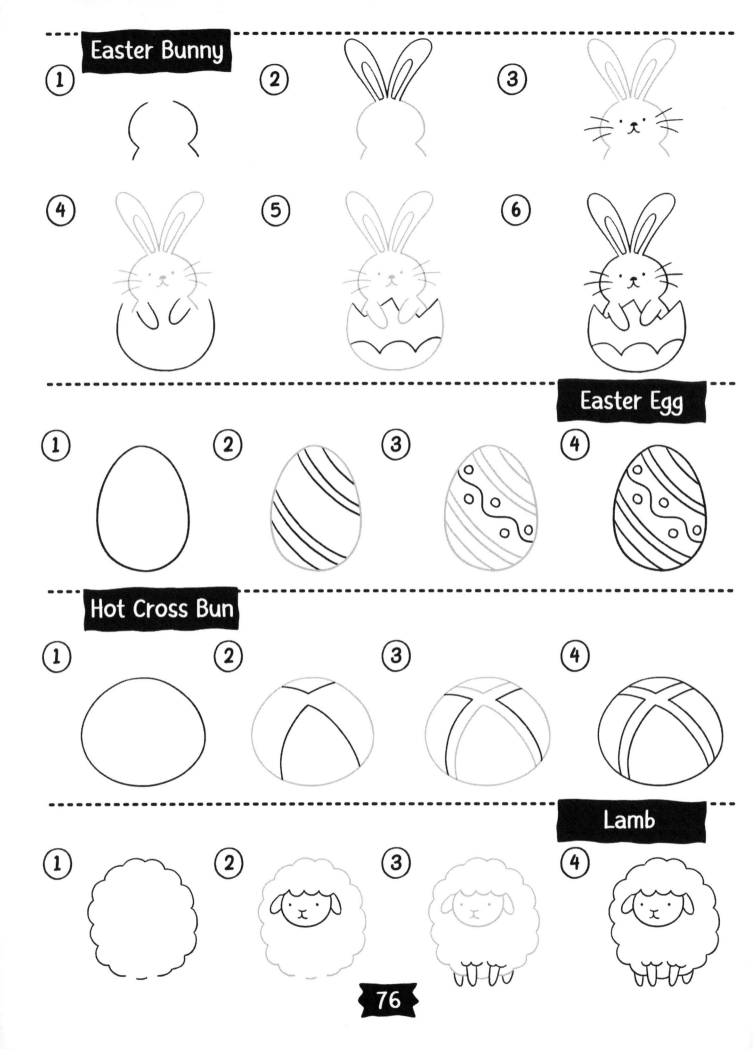

Easter Bunny

① ② ③

④ ⑤ ⑥

Easter Egg

① ② ③ ④

Hot Cross Bun

① ② ③ ④

Lamb

① ② ③ ④

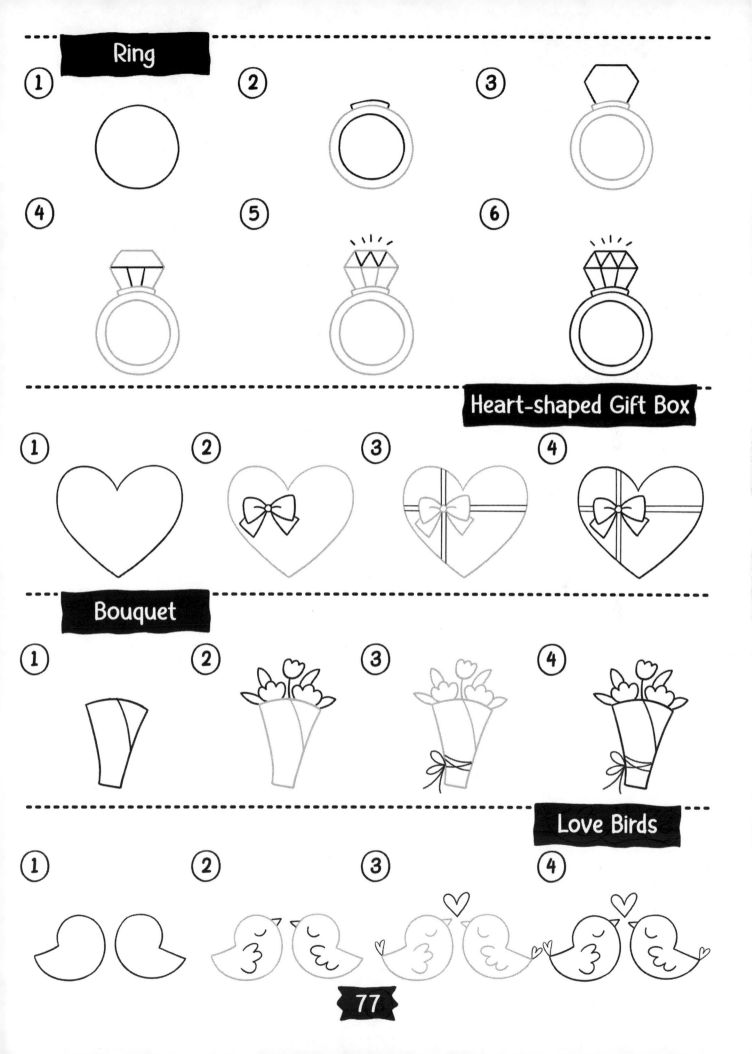

Ring

1
2
3
4
5
6

Heart-shaped Gift Box

1
2
3
4

Bouquet

1
2
3
4

Love Birds

1
2
3
4

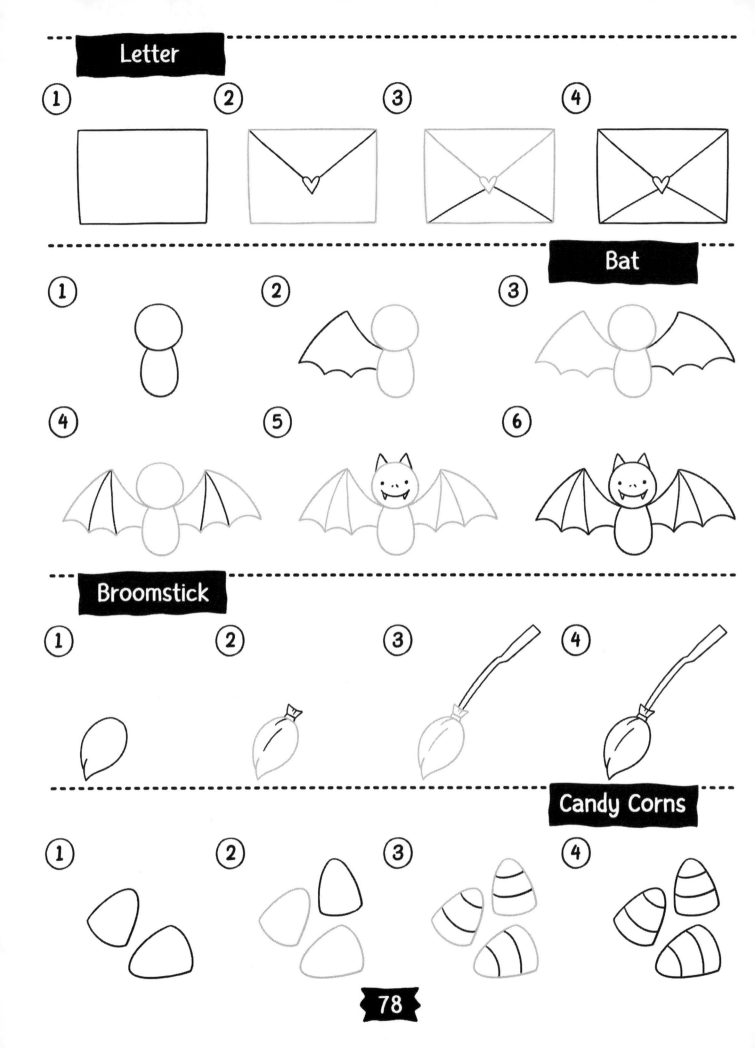

Letter

① ② ③ ④

Bat

① ② ③

④ ⑤ ⑥

Broomstick

① ② ③ ④

Candy Corns

① ② ③ ④

78

Cauldron

① ② ③ ④

Ghost

① ② ③ ④

Jack-o'-lantern

① ② ③

④ ⑤ ⑥

Magic Wand

① ② ③ ④

① ② ③

④ ⑤ ⑥

Potion Bottle

① ② ③

④ ⑤ ⑥

Scarecrow

① ② ③

④ ⑤ ⑥

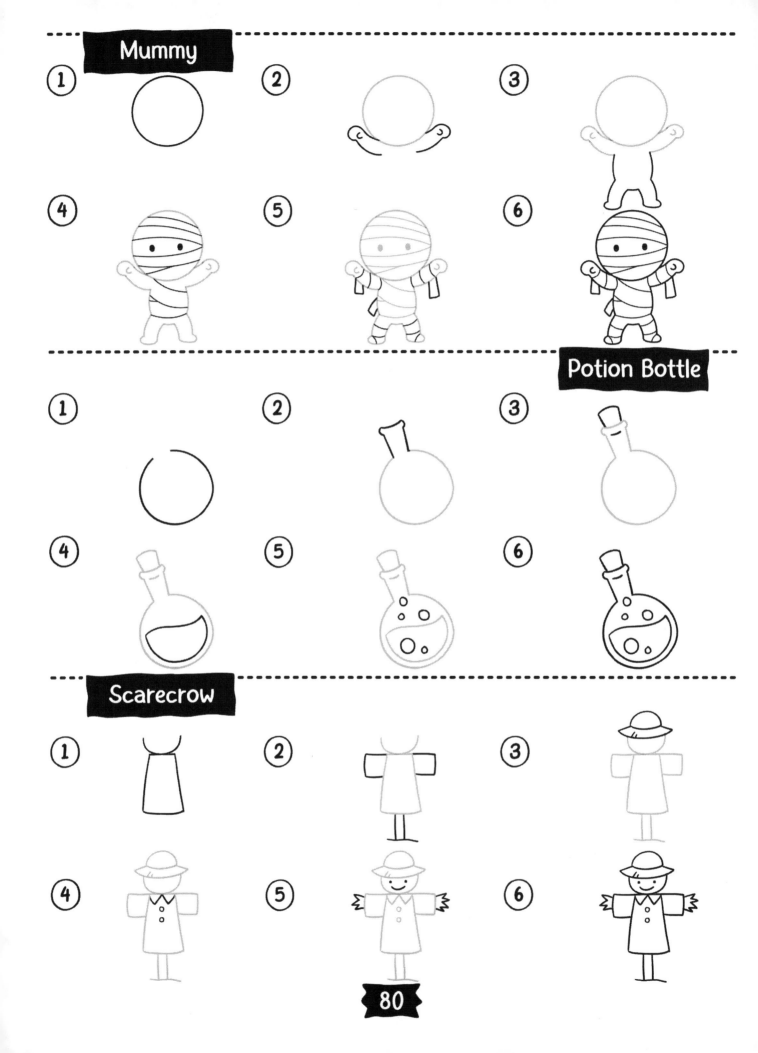

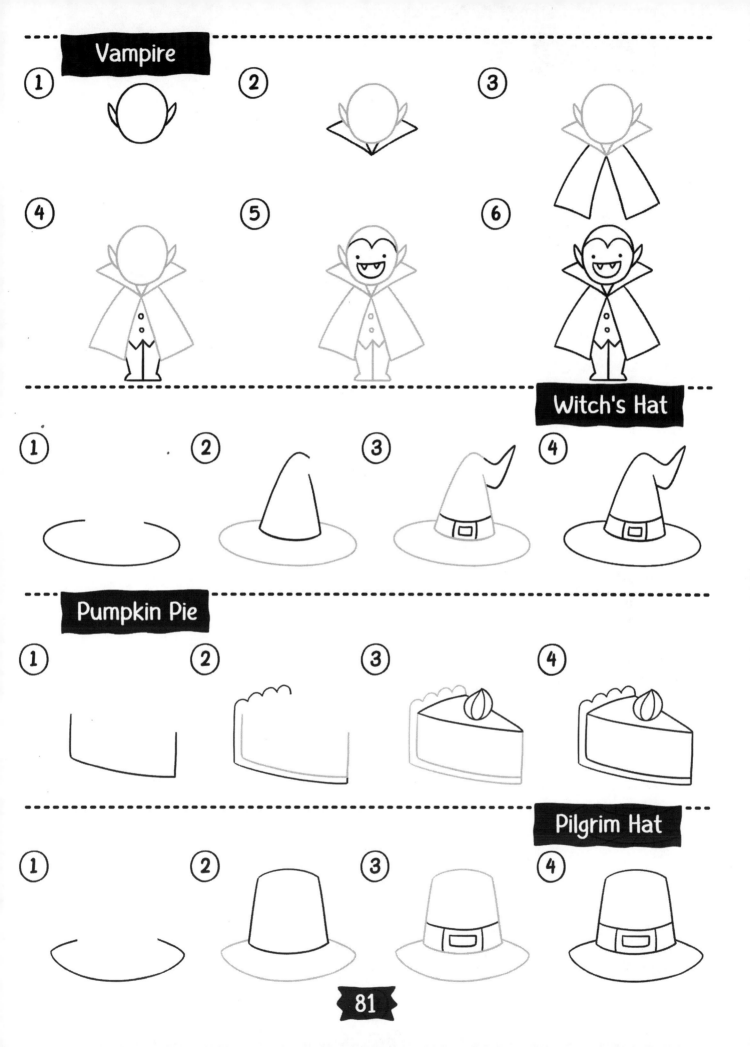

Vampire

① ② ③

④ ⑤ ⑥

Witch's Hat

① ② ③ ④

Pumpkin Pie

① ② ③ ④

Pilgrim Hat

① ② ③ ④

81

Gravy Boat

① ② ③ ④

Roasted Turkey

① ② ③

④ ⑤ ⑥

Bread Rolls

① ② ③ ④

Cinnamon Sticks

① ② ③ ④

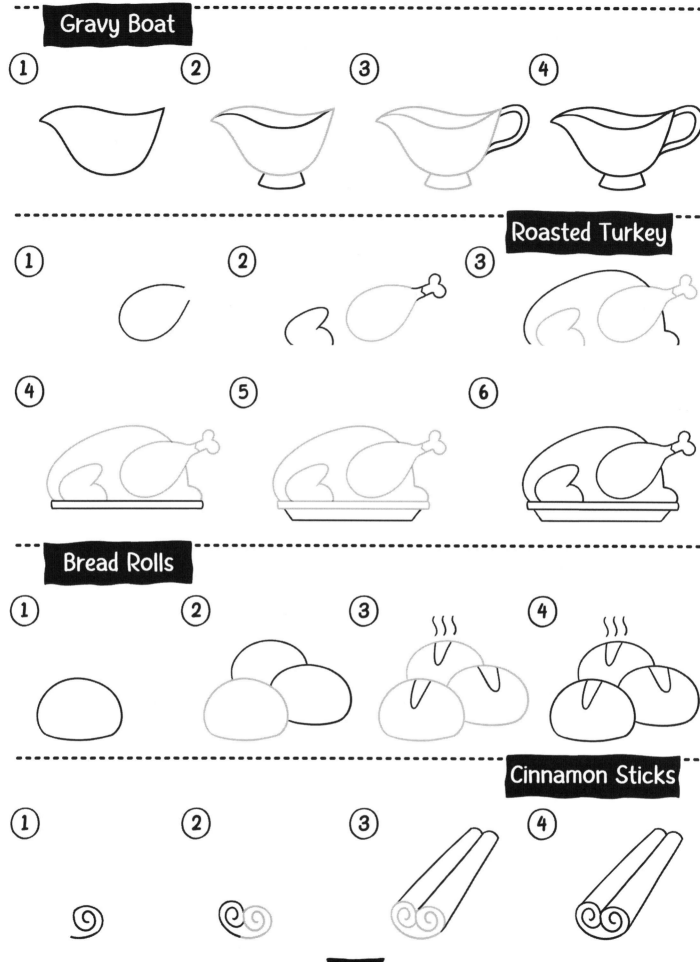

① ② ③ ④

Caramel Apple

① ② ③ ④

Angel

① ② ③ ④

Candy Cane

① ② ③ ④

Chimney

① ② ③ ④

83

Christmas Cracker

① ② ③ ④

Christmas Tree

① ② ③ ④

Elf

① ② ③

④ ⑤ ⑥

Fireplace

① ② ③ ④

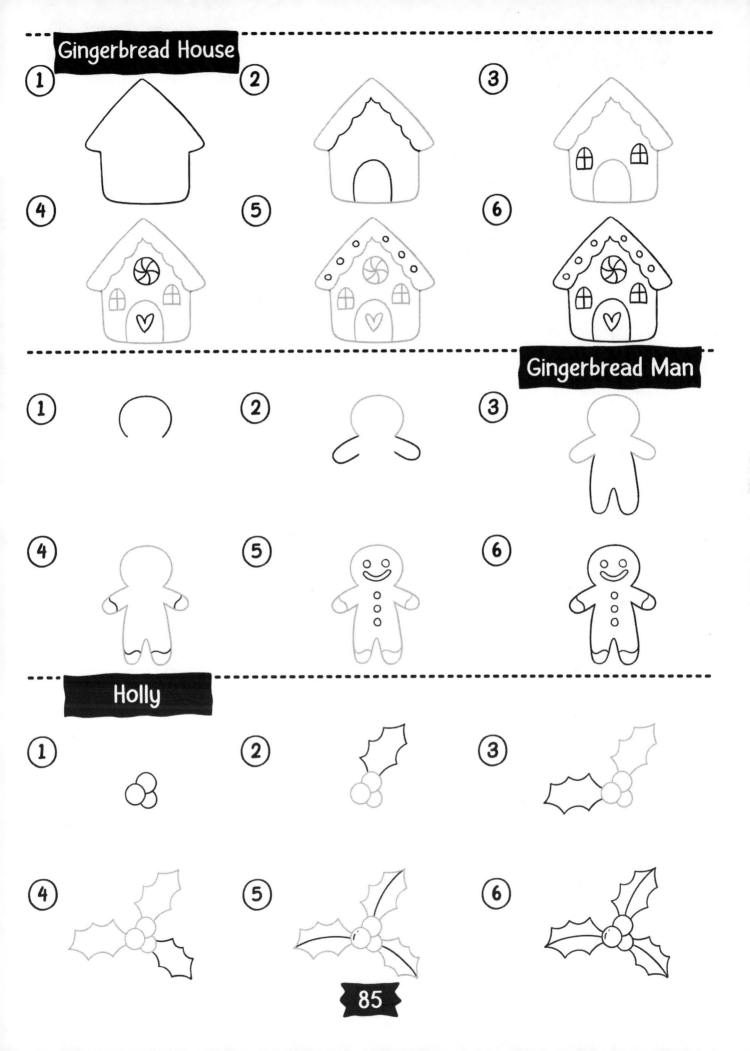

Gingerbread House

① ② ③
④ ⑤ ⑥

Gingerbread Man

① ② ③
④ ⑤ ⑥

Holly

① ② ③
④ ⑤ ⑥

85

Jingle Bells

1

2

3

4

5

6

Mistletoe

1

2

3

4

Ornament

1

2

3

4

Pinecone

1

2

3

4

86

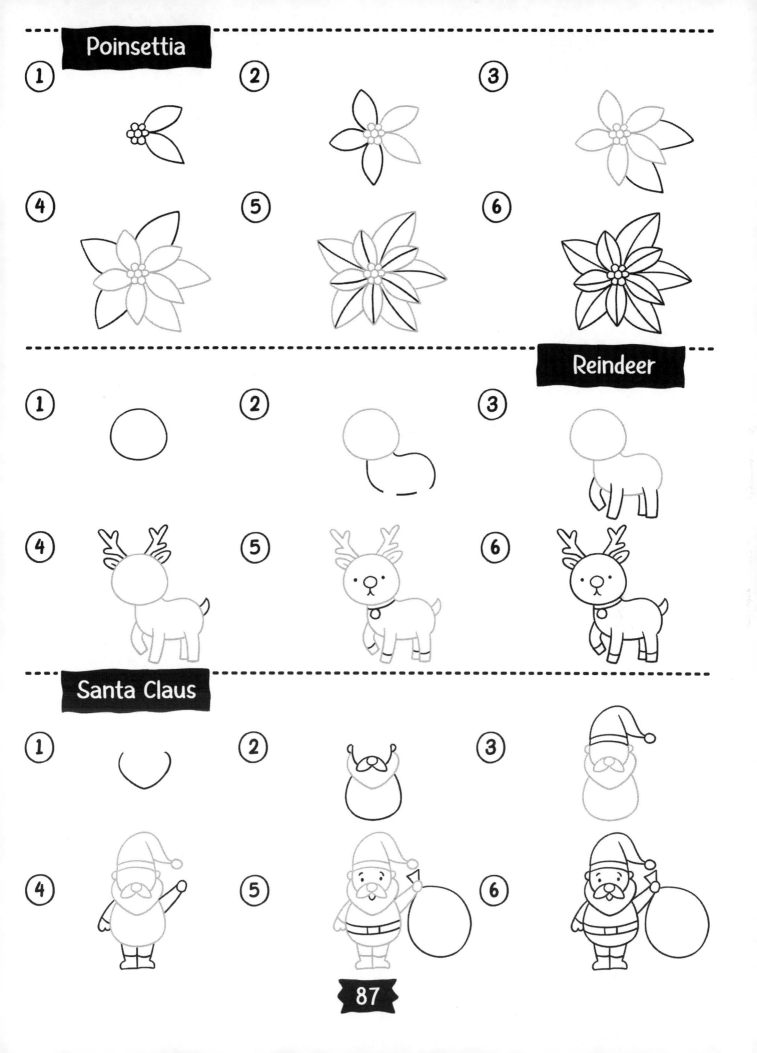

Poinsettia

① ② ③
④ ⑤ ⑥

Reindeer

① ② ③
④ ⑤ ⑥

Santa Claus

① ② ③
④ ⑤ ⑥

Sled

① ② ③ ④

Snow Globe

① ② ③ ④

Snowflake

① ② ③ ④

Snowman

① ② ③

④ ⑤ ⑥

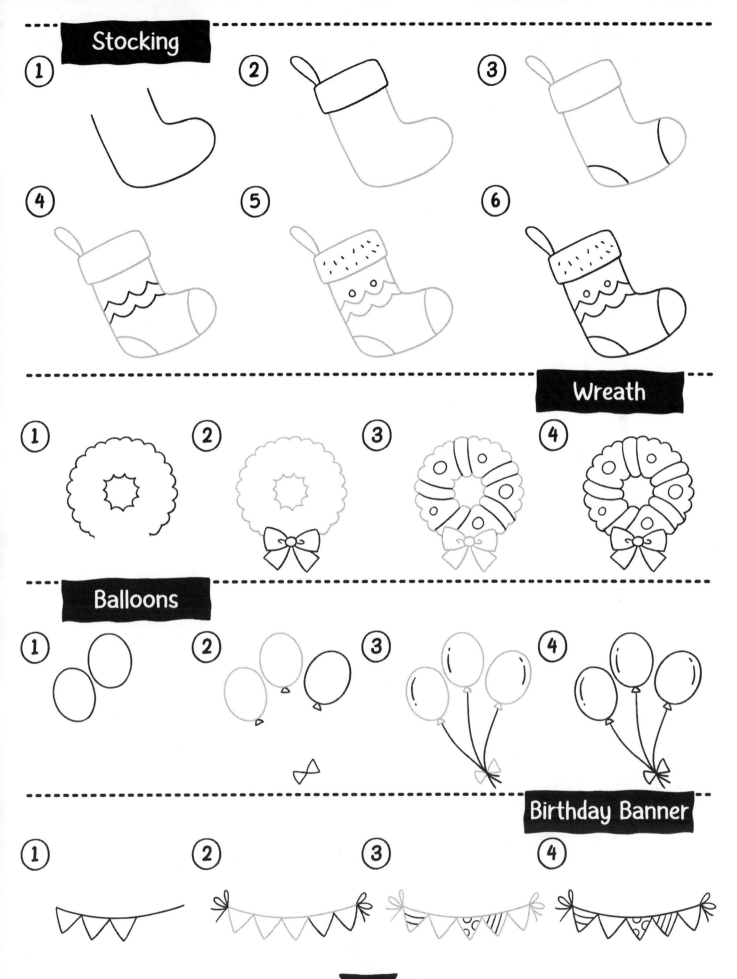

Stocking

Wreath

Balloons

Birthday Banner

89

Birthday Cake

① ② ③

④ ⑤ ⑥

Candle

① ② ③ ④

Gift Box

① ② ③ ④

Gift Card

① ② ③ GIFT CARD ④ GIFT CARD

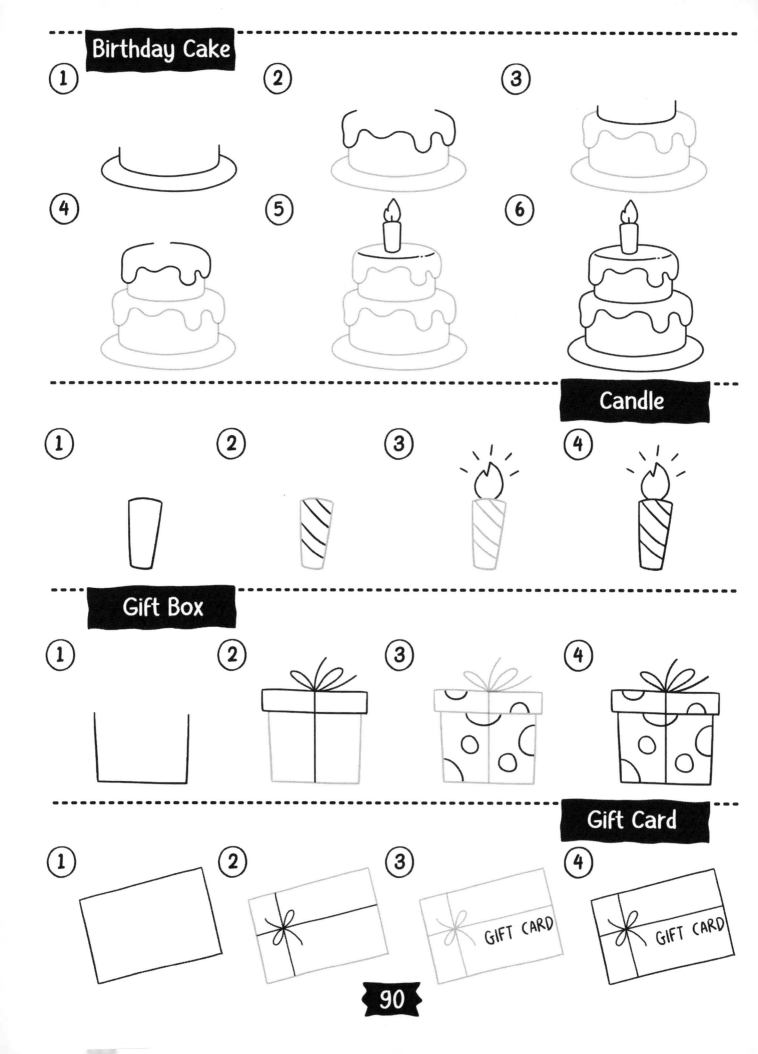

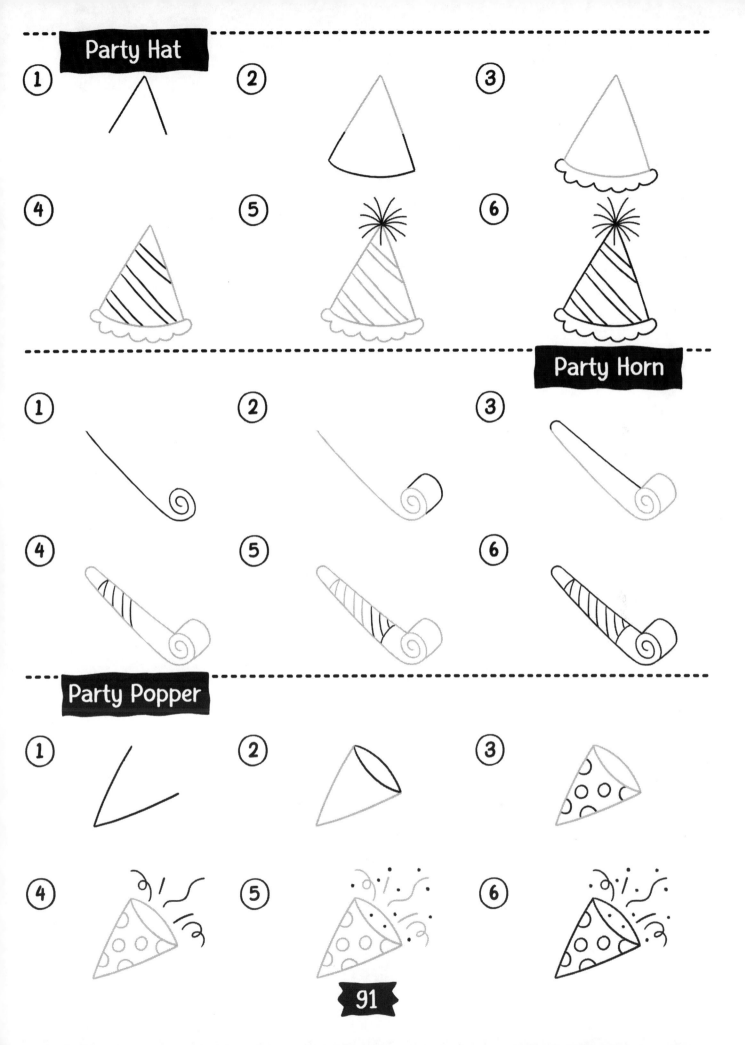

Party Hat

1
2
3
4
5
6

Party Horn

1
2
3
4
5
6

Party Popper

1
2
3
4
5
6

91

① ② ③ ④

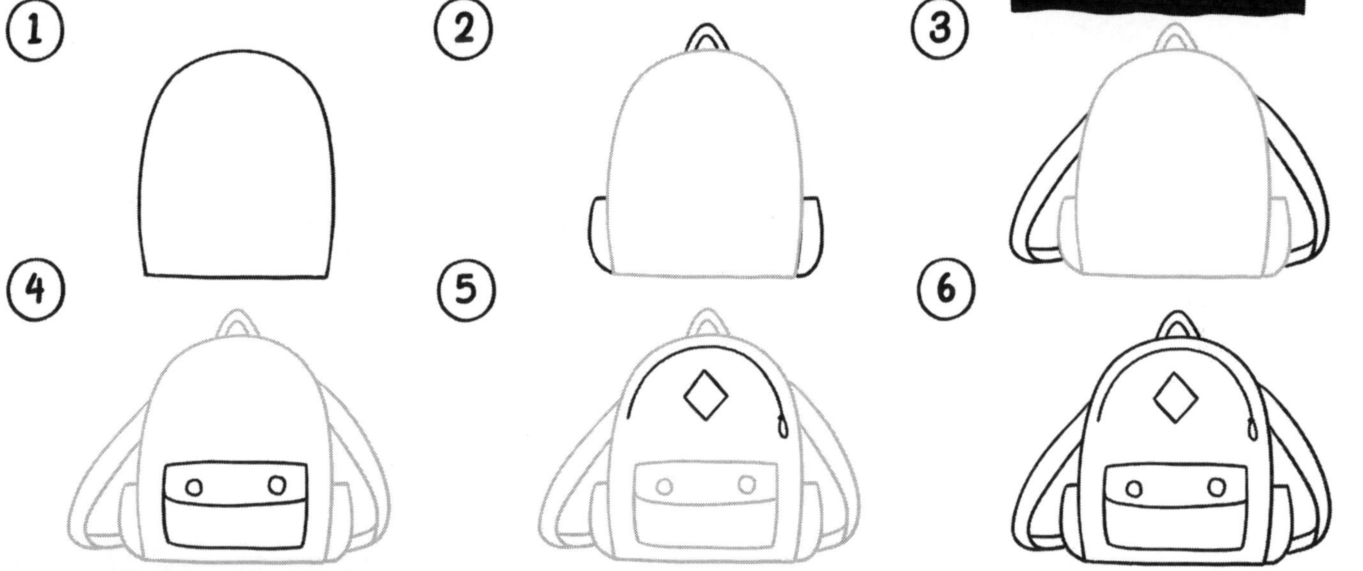

① ② ③

④ ⑤ ⑥

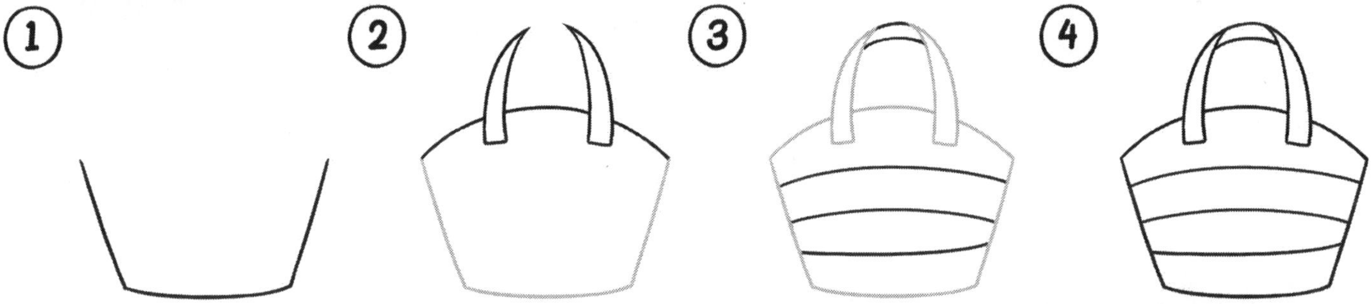

① ② ③ ④

① ② ③ ④

93

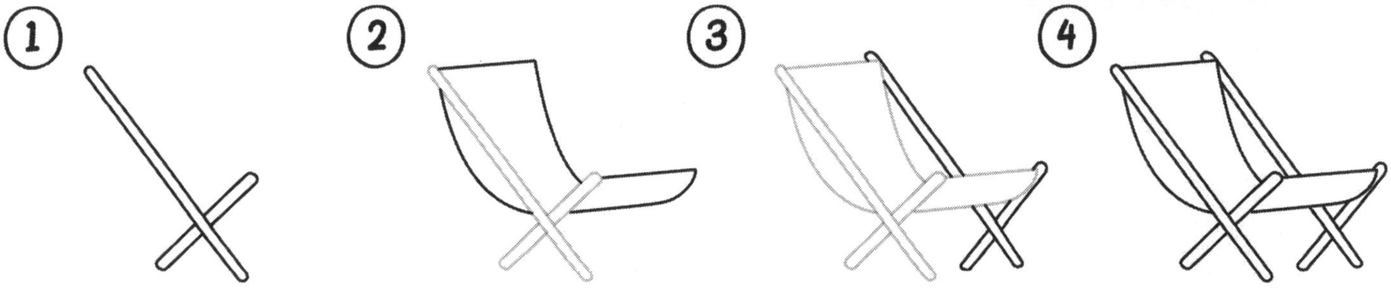

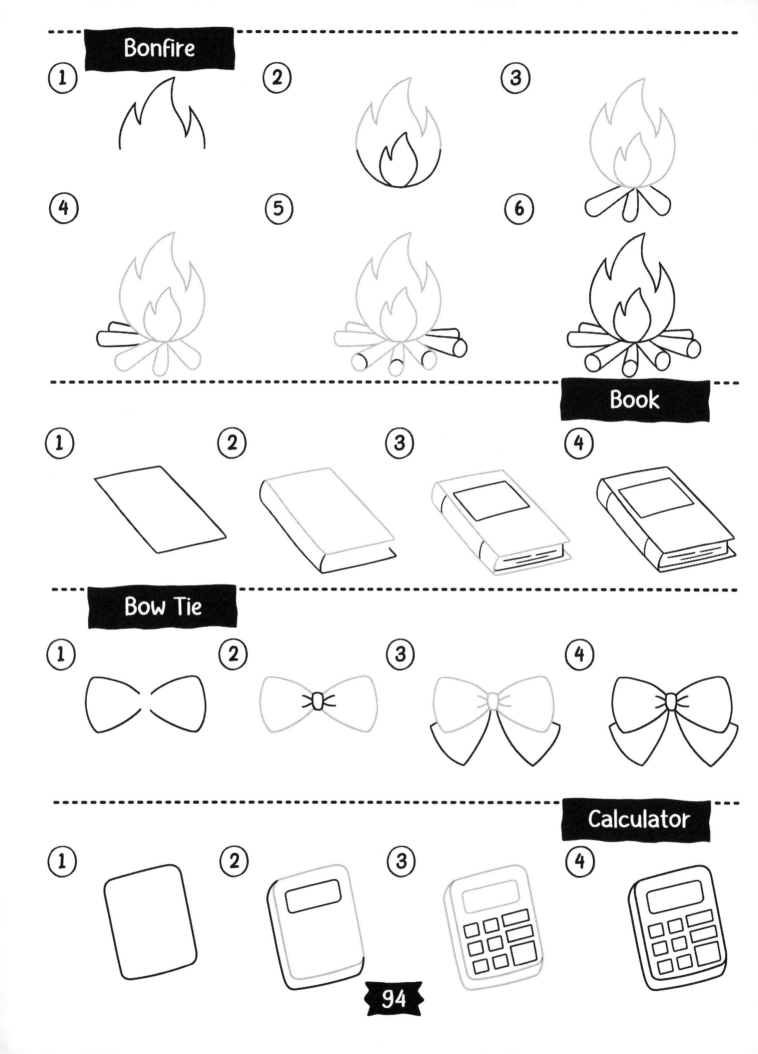

Bonfire

① ② ③

④ ⑤ ⑥

Book

① ② ③ ④

Bow Tie

① ② ③ ④

Calculator

① ② ③ ④

94

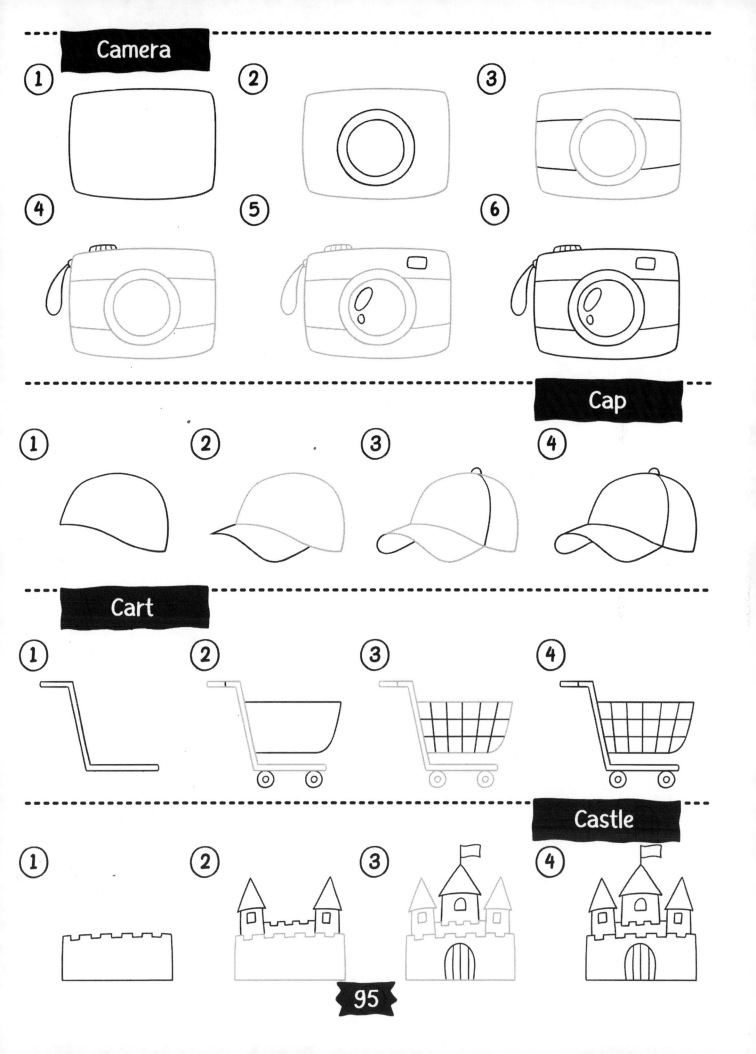

Chef Hat

① ② ③ ④

Clown Hat

① ② ③ ④

Coffee Mug

① ② ③ ④

Crown

① ② ③

④ ⑤ ⑥

96

1 2 3 4

Diamond

1 2 3 4

Dress

1 2 3

4 5 6

Flip Flops

1 2 3 4

97

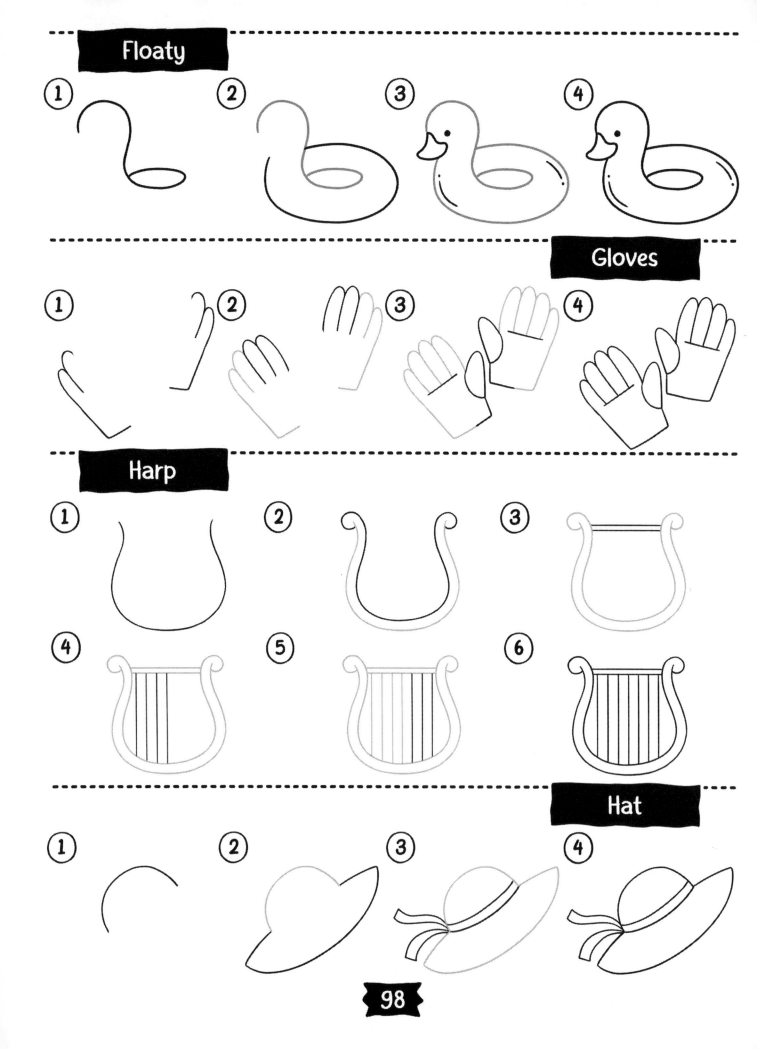

Floaty

① ② ③ ④

Gloves

① ② ③ ④

Harp

① ② ③

④ ⑤ ⑥

Hat

① ② ③ ④

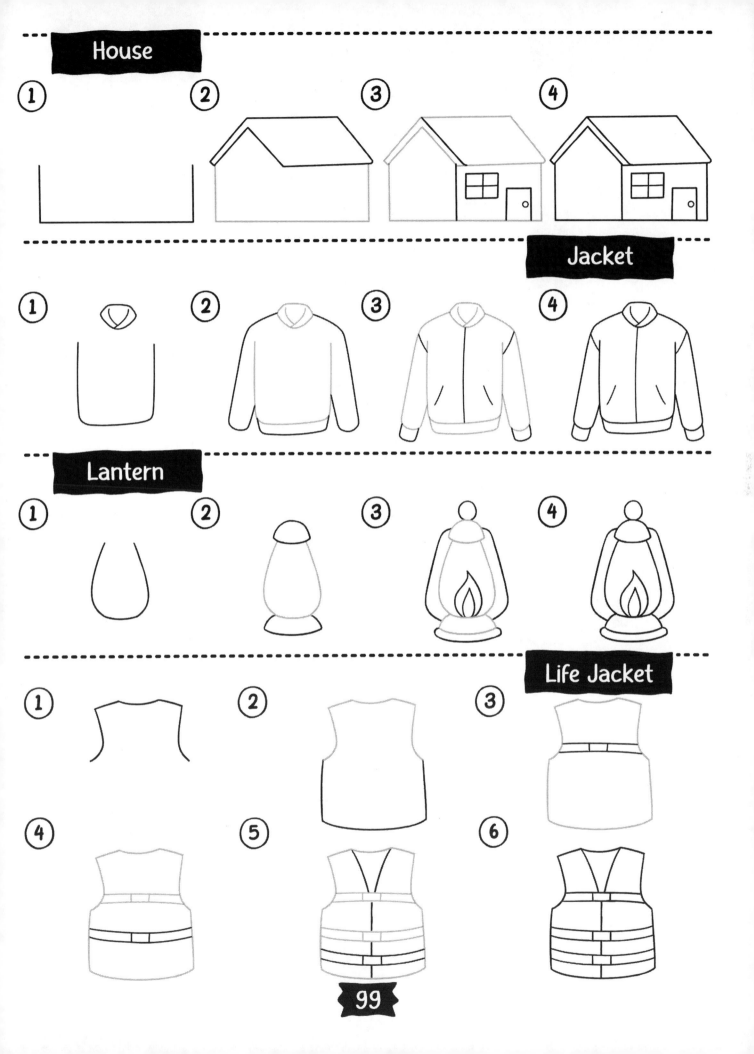

House

① ② ③ ④

Jacket

① ② ③ ④

Lantern

① ② ③ ④

Life Jacket

① ② ③

④ ⑤ ⑥

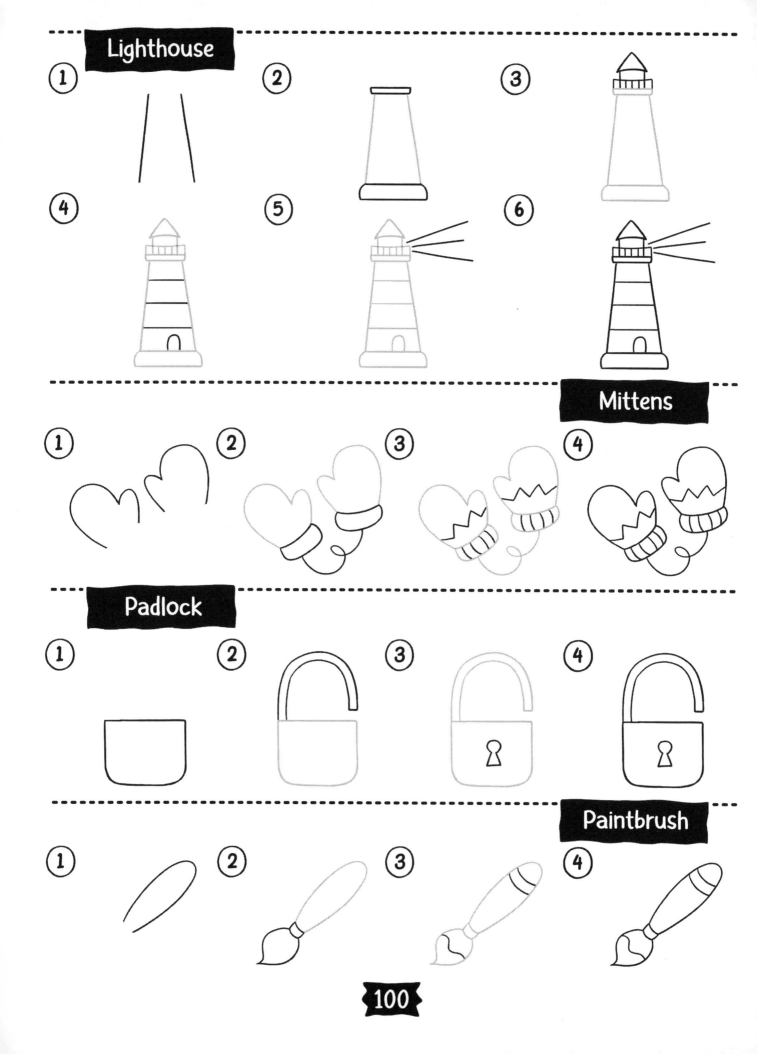

Lighthouse

① ② ③ ④ ⑤ ⑥

Mittens

① ② ③ ④

Padlock

① ② ③ ④

Paintbrush

① ② ③ ④

100

① ② ③ ④

Pet House

① ② ③ ④

Hand Mirror

① ② ③ ④

① ② Picnic Basket ③

④ ⑤ ⑥

1 2 3 4

1 2 3

4 5 6

1 2 3 4

1 2 3 4

① ② ③ ④

① ② ③ ④

① ② ③ ④

① ② ③

④ ⑤ ⑥

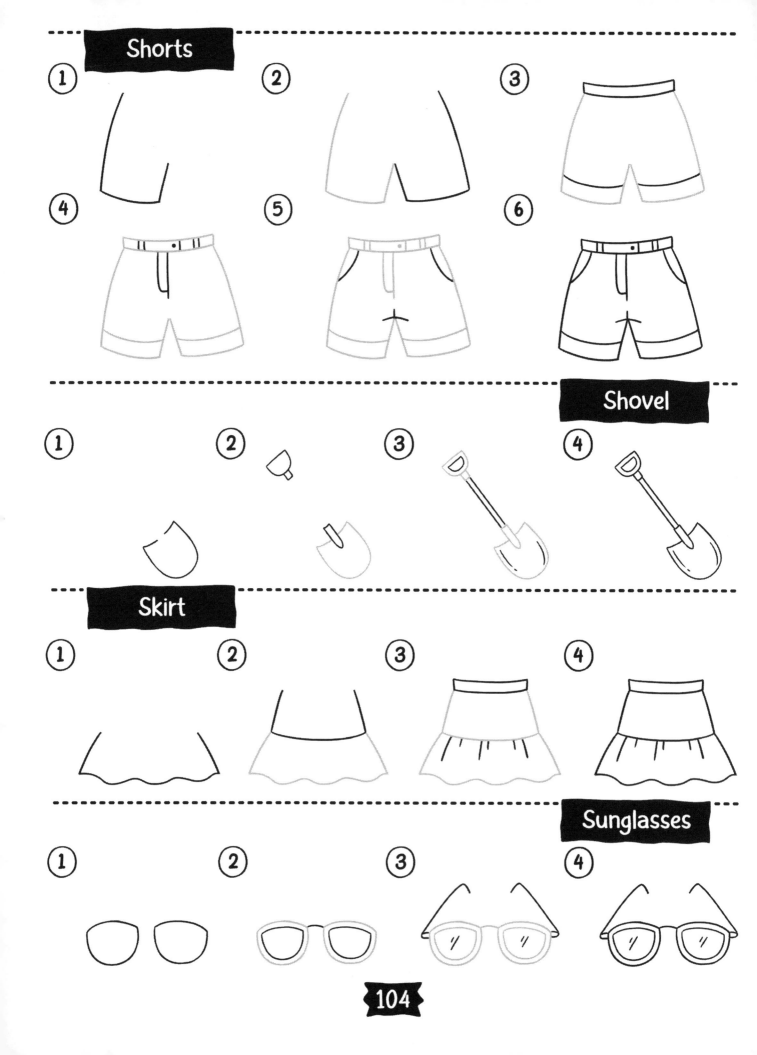

Shorts

① ② ③
④ ⑤ ⑥

Shovel

① ② ③ ④

Skirt

① ② ③ ④

Sunglasses

① ② ③ ④

Sweater

① ② ③ ④

T-Shirt

① ② ③

④ ⑤ ⑥

Tea Cup

① ② ③ ④

Tent

① ② ③ ④

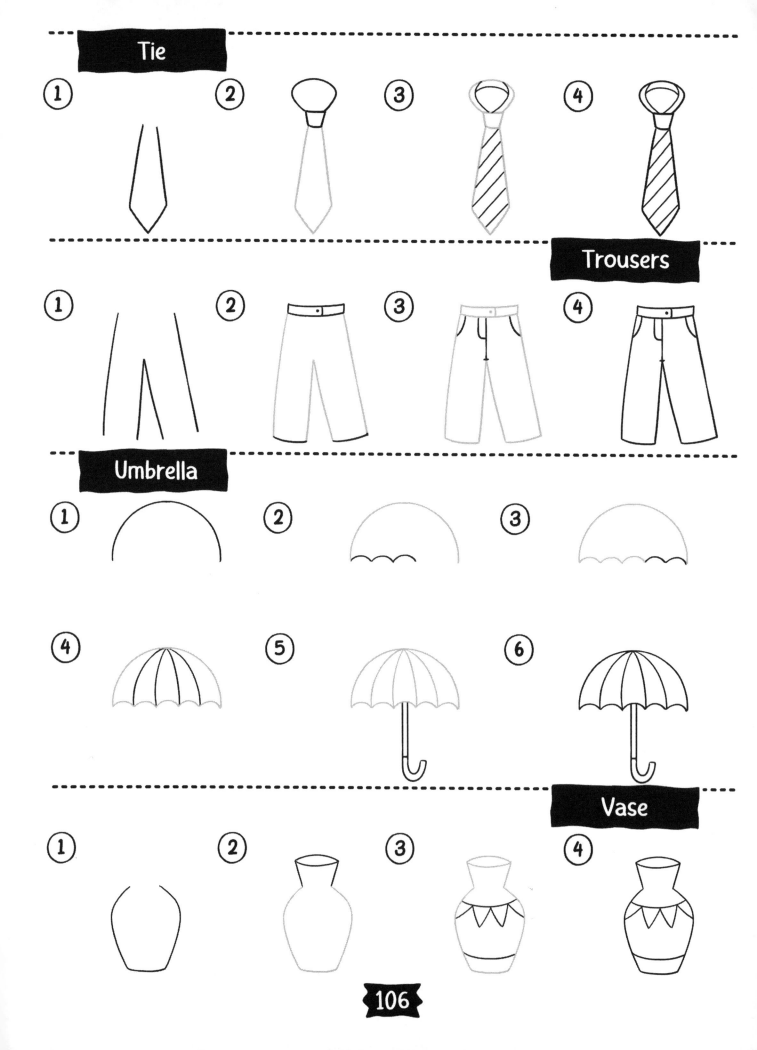

Tie

Trousers

Umbrella

Vase

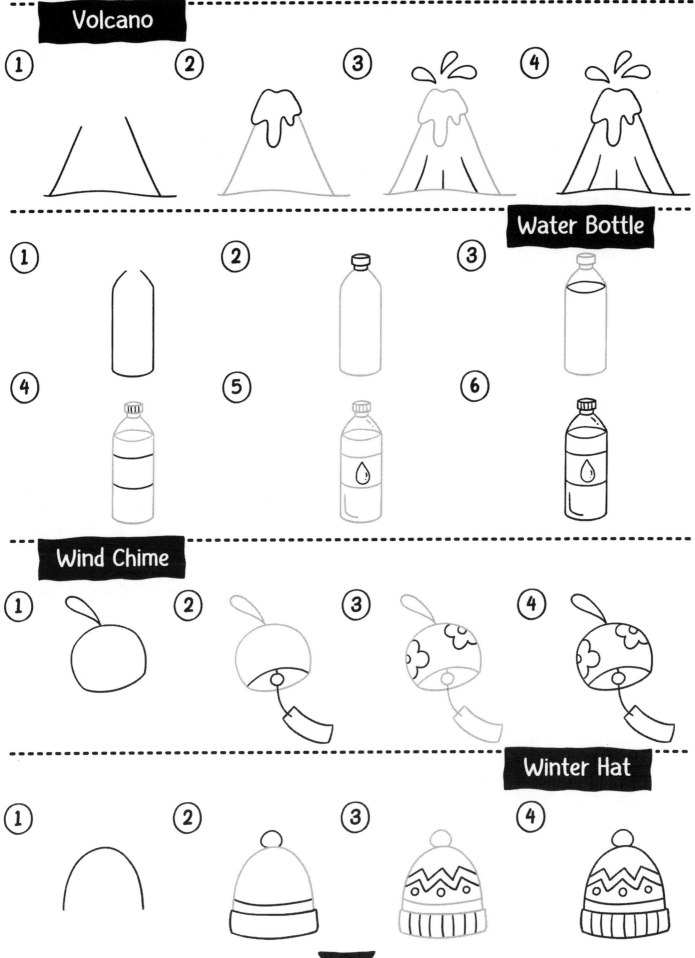

Volcano

① ② ③ ④

Water Bottle

① ② ③

④ ⑤ ⑥

Wind Chime

① ② ③ ④

Winter Hat

① ② ③ ④

Hooray!!! You finished it!

You've completed this incredible drawing guidebook and learned how to draw so many fun things, from cute animals, yummy foods, playful toys, cool vehicles, and many other wonderful things! Keep practicing your new skills by making lots more sketches and let your imagination run wild.

Go ahead, grab your pencil, and keep drawing! I can't wait to see what other beautiful pieces you'll create next.

Congratulations once again and keep it up!

Made in the USA
Columbia, SC
14 December 2024

49267784R00061